Praise for *The S*

"No artifact — in all of history — has held people in thrall the way the Shroud of Turin has. It stakes a mighty claim; but, as Dr. Lavoie demonstrates, an overwhelming preponderance of evidence favors its claim. This book brings all that evidence together, with photos and abundant illustrations, subjecting it to close and dispassionate analysis. The author is always engaging. He never over-reaches. There is no more comprehensive book for those who are curious — or skeptical — about the Shroud."

— **Scott Hahn,** *founder and president,*
St. Paul Center for Biblical Theology

"This is a veritable summa of Shroud studies, incorporating evidence from disciplines as diverse as botany and history, chemistry and theology, Judaic studies and forensic science. It leaves no stitch unexamined, no stones of history unturned. Over the course of decades, Dr. Lavoie has tested every objection to the Shroud's authenticity. He details his findings here without ever bogging the narrative. The book would be a page-turner if only the photos weren't so riveting! You'll want to stop and examine every one."

— **Mike Aquilina,** *author,*
The Fathers of the Church *and* **The Apostles and Their Times**

"This book offers Dr. Lavoie's own scrupulous detective work built especially on his knowledge, as a physician, of the human body both in life and death. And truly the book does read like a detective mystery with persistent analysis and reanalysis, with hypotheses tested by experimentation, with surprising new insights and with a stunning conclusion."

— **Rev. Jurgen Liias,**
Priest of the Ordinariate of the Chair of St. Peter

"This fascinating book uses modern science to examine and validate an astonishing Biblical claim."

— **Lynette Lewis,**
Emmy-Award-Winning Television Producer

THE SHROUD OF JESUS

Gilbert R. Lavoie, M.D.

THE SHROUD OF JESUS

And the Sign John Ingeniously Concealed

SOPHIA INSTITUTE PRESS

Manchester, New Hampshire

Sophia Institute Press
Box 5284, Manchester, NH 03108
1-800-888-9344
www.SophiaInstitute.com

Sophia Institute Press is a registered trademark of Sophia Institute.

Print edition ISBN: 978-1-64413-886-1

Electronic formats ISBN: 978-1-64413-887-8

Library of Congress Control Number: 2023935990

2nd Printing

Contents

◇◇◇◇◇◇◇◇◇

THE SHROUD OF JESUS

◇◇◇◇◇◇◇◇◇

Chapter 1

Introduction

IT ALL STARTED in an old bookstore in downtown Boston. There I picked up a book called *A Doctor at Calvary*. It was a story that a French surgeon, Dr. Pierre Barbet, had written, and the only reason I picked it up was that I was then in pre-med, and I thought it would be the surgeon's version of Jesus' crucifixion. But it was more than that. It was about Jesus' burial cloth, of which I had never heard. Seventeen years later, just as I started to read the *Boston Sunday Globe*, I saw the picture of this same cloth, the Shroud of Turin. It was 1978 and it was then, as a young physician and a young skeptic, that I began this pursuit, always seeking the truth. And in the end, I came to an astonishing realization. It took a lifetime.

For all who wonder if there is a God at work, if there is a spiritual world, if there is everlasting life, if there is a God who is true, keep wondering and keep reading.

Please join me on a journey, an adventure I never sought and barely knew I was on. Only in time did I realize its joy. With your own eyes and your own mind, simply look and observe and come to realize what the image and blood marks of this cloth reveal. Now join this old physician for a few hours and start this adventure of discovery by first looking at forensic medical evidence that took me years to fully comprehend. And that is just the beginning of the story.

The first part of my forty-year journey deals with the forensics of the visual objective reality of the controversial Shroud of Turin located in Turin, Italy, at the Cathedral of San Giovanni Battista (Turin Cathedral) since 1578. It is a linen cloth made from flax, approximately 14 feet by 3.5 feet, that carries a faint image of the back and front of a naked man. It also carries blood marks that are consistent with the scourging and crucifixion of Jesus of Nazareth as described in the Gospel of John. Many believe that it is Jesus' burial cloth, and many do not. Figure 1.1 below shows the full shroud, followed by the frontal image, figure 1.2, and back image, figure 1.3, of the man of the shroud. (Note: In this text, both the back and front images together are sometimes referred to as the image of the shroud.)

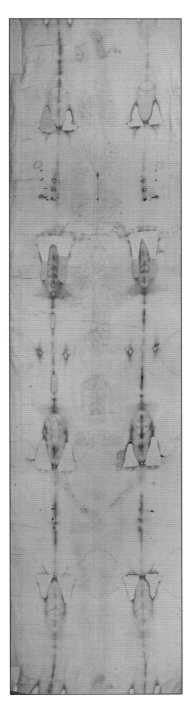

Figure 1.1: Full-color image of the shroud

Note, the back (upper) and front (lower) of a faint body image can be seen along the central length of the cloth. The two brown parallel lines and patches along each side of the body image are the result of a fire that occurred in Chambery, France in 1532.

The crucified man was placed on his back (supine) on one end of this cloth, and the other end was placed over his body.

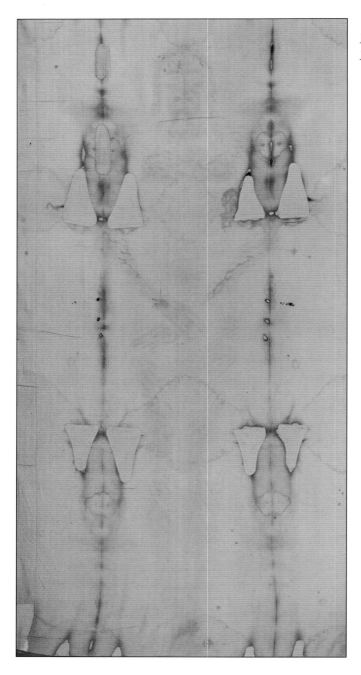

Figure 1.2:
Frontal Image

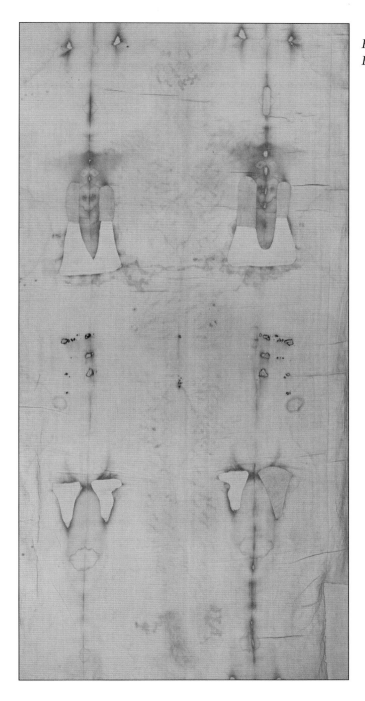

Figure 1.3:
Back Image

What I visually discovered about the image of the shroud eventually brought me to the second part of my journey: I began to delve deeply into the study of the Gospel of John. There I found that by placing what I forensically observed on this cloth into the context of Jesus' life, a door opened into new insights as to what John had written about Jesus. The image on the shroud was the key that opened that door. And then gradually, because of what is visible on the shroud cloth, I began to uncover the message that the shroud holds for us.

The Authenticity of the Shroud Is in Doubt — Why Study It?

There have been four major reasons that have brought doubt that the shroud is the burial cloth of Jesus. The first is that it has been stated to be a medieval work of art. However, one can come to readily appreciate that the shroud's blood marks and image are not a work of art because of the many studies that have been done (see in chapter 5), including the studies visually evident throughout this book.

The second reason for doubt is that while the shroud cloth's written history documenting its location is well known all the way back to the 1350s, in contrast, before the 1350s the historical documents leading back to the time of Jesus do not provide a "chain of custody." Yet new historic research continues to fill the gaps, revealing where the shroud has been over time, though much remains incomplete. [For more on history, see note 1.1.]

There is visual objective evidence, however, that helps fill in the paucity of historical data documenting the shroud's location prior to the 1350s. Two important discoveries, one botanical and one archeological, have provided this visual evidence. In the area of botany there was the discovery of microscopic pollen spores on the shroud that was made in the 1970s by Dr. Max Frei, a professor of criminology from the University of Zurich. He was a biologist who made a specialty of using microscopic techniques in the field of criminology. He not only confirms that the shroud cloth was in Europe, but his pollen study gives it a pre-European itinerary documenting that the shroud had also been in the locations of Asia Minor and Palestine/Jerusalem where Jesus lived. See an example of a pollen spore taken from the shroud in figure 1.4. [For more on Dr. Max Frei and his pollen study, see note 1.2.]

Figure 1.4: Pollen grain of Phillyrea angustifolia

Pollen grain found in dust vacuumed from the shroud. It comes from "an evergreen plant that flowers between March and May and adapts well to the difficult terrain of some Mediterranean areas that are characterized by extreme drought. This type of pollen was just the type classified by Frei in his work." (see note 1.2, ref. 6)

The second discovery of visual objective data pointing to one of the shroud's pre-European locations was the archeological evidence discovered by the textile expert and historian Mechthild Flury-Lemberg. She did the major textile restoration of the Shroud of Turin in 2002 and discovered a unique stitch that was used to sew together two original sections of the shroud cloth. Because of this distinctive stitch done by hand, there is a high probability that the shroud cloth was previously located in Palestine sometime before AD 74 (figures 1.5, 1.6). The unique sewing technique that stitched together the two original pieces of shroud cloth is comparable to stitches found among cloth fragments from antiquity. These cloth fragments with the same stitch were discovered in the Jewish fortress city of Masada, within a three-day walk from Jerusalem. Masada fell to the Roman army in AD 73. The discovery of this distinctive stitch pointing to a time and general location where the shroud cloth had been at some time in the past (as revealed in the pollen study) is archeological evidence that cannot be ignored. [For more on textile evidence, see note 1.3.]

*Figure 1.5: Black-
and-white photo of
the lower back side of
the shroud image*

Note the two black arrows. They
point to the seam connecting a
long strip of cloth that has been
added to the shroud. It runs the
whole length of the cloth. At
the lower left bottom, note that
a patch of that strip has been
removed at some unknown time
in the past.

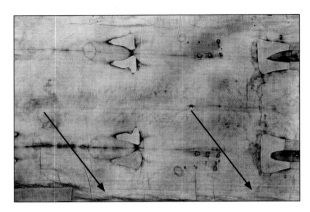

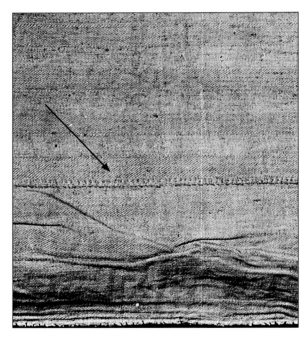

*Figure 1.6: Close-up of
the seam of the long strip
of cloth added to the full
length of the shroud*

The black arrow points to
the seam connecting this long
narrow strip to the full-size
shroud. The stitching of the
seam is unique in that among
ancient textiles the only one like
it has been found in Masada,
within a three-day walk from
Jerusalem. Masada fell to the
Roman army in AD 73. Note
that the herringbone weave of
both sections of the cloth above
and below the stitched seam are
identical. Therefore, this long
narrow piece of fabric is identical
to the larger piece, and this
stitching was likely done around
the time that this fine linen cloth,
made of flax, was used as a
burial shroud.

The third reason for doubt is that a carbon dating study done in 1988 concluded that the shroud cloth originated in the fourteenth century (1260–1390). That study has remained controversial for many reasons. [For more on carbon dating, see note 1.4.]

Recently, the shroud cloth has been dated by four new methods that have not been as well publicized as carbon dating. From the analysis of the first three different methods combined, the final date of the shroud cloth calculates to 33 BC plus or minus 250 years. That time span includes the time frame of Jesus' life. [For more on the first three dating methods, see note 1.5.]

The fourth and most recent test is a new X-ray dating method demonstrating that the Turin Shroud linen sample measurements are "fully compatible with analogous [similar] measurements obtained on a linen sample whose dating, by historical records, is 55–74 AD, Siege of Masada (Israel)."[1] Indeed, from the data provided by these four tests, the shroud cloth is two thousand years old. [For more on the fourth and most recent test, see note 1.6.]

Finally, the fourth reason for doubt is that there is no mention in any of the Gospels that there was an image of Jesus on his shroud. The reason for this very intentional silence will be addressed in this book.

Place and time are fundamental to documenting the authenticity of the shroud. The pollen data and archeological textile data that can be visualized do not point to a European origin but present pre-European places where this shroud had been, and one of them is Palestine. The four dating methods point to the first century as its time of origin. But most essential is the challenge of establishing who the person is who was buried in this cloth. To begin, we will study what everyone in the world can easily see, the blood marks and the inexplicable image of the man of the shroud.

Later we will study the Gospel of John. The Gospels can stand on their own, but the shroud without the Gospel of John — or indeed without the other three Gospels — would simply be a cloth with the blood stains and image of a man who was scourged, crowned with thorns, and crucified. The blood marks and the image of the crucified naked man would be fascinating, but it would all stop there, as it would not be related to any consequential events of the past. However, the Gospel of John makes the shroud an object of discovery in that there are past events that could explain its existence. Moreover, if the shroud can be judged to be the burial cloth of Jesus, then this cloth with its image and blood marks would have existed before all the Gospels were written. And, if that were the case, then the question is, what effect, if any, would this have had on the writer of the Gospel of John? This, in part, is what we are about to explore.

We are going to concentrate on the Gospel of John as opposed to the other three Gospels, Matthew, Mark, and Luke (called the Synoptic Gospels, which carry definite common relationships). The Gospel of John is unique and gives much objective data that causes one to seriously consider that John was aware of this burial cloth with its image and blood marks. The other three Gospel writers, other than mentioning a burial cloth and the passion of Jesus, do not give the impression that they were as aware of this same cloth as was John, the on-site witness.

The purpose of this book is to present a deeper understanding of the extraordinary events that the blood and image on the shroud reveal. This examination rests mainly on visual, forensic science that you can see. Equipped with this data, you will be able to decide for yourself if Jesus and the man of the shroud are the same person. The relationship between the Gospel of John and the Shroud of Turin will become self-evident as we move forward. My objective is to show that this cloth is part of an astonishing event that corresponds with the words, works, and life of Jesus of Nazareth as recorded in John's Gospel.

◇◇◇◇◇◇◇◇◇

CHAPTER 2

Discovery: The Hidden Image

THE NINETEENTH CENTURY issued in a new era of technology: photography. By 1898 the first official photograph of the Shroud of Turin was taken by Secondo Pia, an Italian lawyer and amateur photographer. It was during the development of Pia's photographs of the shroud, in the quiet of his darkroom, that he saw something on his black-and-white negative photo that not only astounded him but changed forever the understanding of the faint image of the man of the shroud. The image on

Figure 2.1: Black-and-white photo (note the mirror image)

Positive photo of shroud cloth with   *Negative photo of shroud cloth*
negative image of a man   *with positive image of a man*

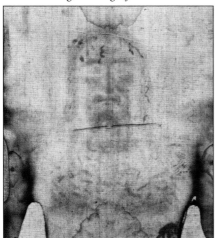 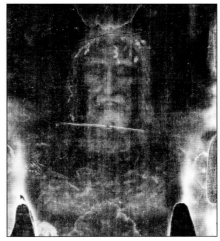

the photographic negative was not the negative image that he expected. Rather, it was the positive image of a man. The awareness that his negative held the positive image of a man brought him to another realization: the image on the shroud cloth is a negative[1] (figures 2.1, 2.2, 2.3). That discovery of the hidden positive image of the man of the shroud brought a whole new perspective to the study of this cloth.

Figure 2.2: Positive photo of shroud cloth with negative image of a man

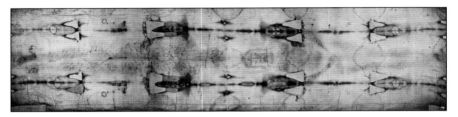

Figure 2.3: Negative photo of shroud cloth with positive image of a man

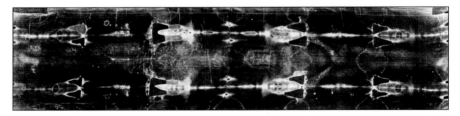

Many studies of this cloth took place over the following years, and by 1978 a scientific investigation called the Shroud of Turin Research Project of 1978 (STURP) took place in Turin, Italy (more on STURP in chapter 5). The chief scientific photographer was Vernon Miller, world-renowned for his work. His shroud photographs are shown throughout this book. They show the burned-area patches from the 1532 fire.[2] These patches were removed during the restoration of 2002.

As for the image of the man of the shroud, it is as Vernon Miller stated: "It took the camera, with its negative image [photo], to appreciate it."[3] Comparing the shroud as it appears to the naked eye (see colored film, figure 2.4) to the black-and-white negative film (figure 2.4), we can see that it is only from the negative photo of the black-and-white film that we are able to appreciate the definite positive view of the man of the shroud.

Note that the blood marks are negative on the black-and-white photo with its "positive" image, but the blood marks are positive on the original cloth with its "negative" image (figure 2.4). More on Vernon Miller's photography of the Turin Shroud will be found in chapter 5.

Figure 2.4: Color and black-and-white photos of the center of the shroud image, back and front of head and chest (note blood marks)

Positive color photo of shroud cloth negative image, blood marks positive

Negative black-and-white photo of shroud cloth positive image, blood marks negative

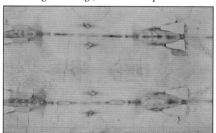
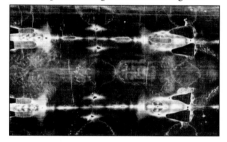

Yes, the Shroud of Turin is unique in the world. It is the only ancient textile known to display the blood marks of a crucifixion. But even more astonishing, this cloth also displays the negative image of a naked man who was crucified. With black-and-white photography, we now see the true positive likeness of his image, which has been hidden in its original negative form for centuries. These photos led many researchers and nonscientists alike to want to know more.

CHAPTER 3

The Gospel of John and the Blood Marks on the Shroud

LET'S BEGIN OUR search for answers about who God is by first reading about what John saw on the day that Jesus died and compare it to what we see on the Turin Shroud. Most of us like a good mystery and are naturally curious, wanting to see how the forensic experts unravel what happened at the scene of a homicide. In many such stories, the criminal is caught because he or she slips up and divulges the details of how a crime was committed or confesses to a crime. The investigators sometimes realize that the person is either a witness or the perpetrator, for he or she would be the only one to know the specific details discovered at the crime scene. Starting from this perspective, what is most evident on the burial cloth of the Shroud of Turin is the brutal treatment that the crucified man endured. So the question is, did John, our Gospel witness, give us any details that tell us that the man of the shroud and Jesus are likely the same person?

We will start with the events that led up to the crucifixion and death of Jesus. According to John's witness, it was close to the time of the Passover, and Jesus and his disciples were in Jerusalem. After supper, they went out "across the Kidron valley to a place where there was a garden" (John 18:1). There Jesus was arrested by Roman soldiers and the Jewish police. And who led them there? It was his disciple Judas, who betrayed him. During that same night, Jesus was brought before Caiaphas, the Jewish high priest, and by morning, the day before Passover, they took Jesus to the headquarters of Pilate, the Roman leader of Judea.

The events of this day are centered on the accused, Jesus, who is on trial; the judge, who is Pilate; Jesus' accusers, who are the Jewish religious leaders; and the observing and shouting crowd. What proceeds is the drama of Pilate asking what

Jesus is accused of. The Jewish religious leaders accuse him of claiming to be the Son of God — blasphemy — and at the same time they accuse him of claiming to be the King of the Jews — treason (John, chapters 18 and 19).

After questioning Jesus, Pilate said to the Jews, "I find no case against him. But you have a custom that I release someone for you at the Passover. Do you want me to release for you the King of the Jews?" They shouted in reply, "Not this man" (John 18:38–40). "Then Pilate took Jesus and had him flogged" (John 19:1). Flogging is a beating of the flesh that inflicts scourge marks that can be seen, on the back and front, from the upper torso down to the lower legs of the man of the shroud.

I first read about these scourge marks many years ago. They were well described by the French surgeon, Dr. Barbet, who studied the shroud in the 1930s and 1940s. His objective forensic description was superb.[1] On the man of the shroud, the scourge marks of the skin (wounds) are in pairs and are dumbbell in shape. In Barbet's words, "The two circles represent the balls of lead, while the line joining them is the mark of the thong."[2] Barbet found that most of these wounds are in parallel pairs. From this observation, Barbet deduced that the instrument of scourging had two thongs. These marks per Barbet appear to correspond to the design of a Roman flagrum. The flagrum was made of a handle from which extended two

Figure 3.1: Scourge marks in pairs and dumbbell in shape

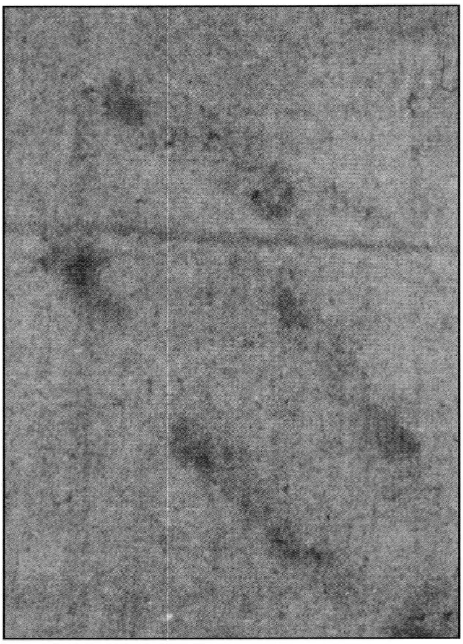

Ultraviolet-light-enhanced scourge marks, see figure 3.12

or more long leather straps that held bone or lead on their ends. These ends were dumbbell in shape and were designed to pick out flesh from the victim (figure 3.1). In the following color photo, notice the scourge marks that extend from the low back down to the lower legs of the man of the shroud (figure 3.2). These scourge marks are all over the body but are best seen on the back image in the following black-and-white photo (figure 3.3).

Figure 3.2: Scourge marks from the low back down to the lower legs

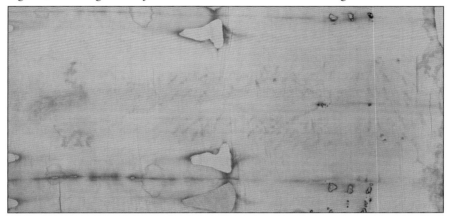

Figure 3.3: Black-and-white negative photo of the back image
Note the scourge marks from the upper back down to the lower legs.

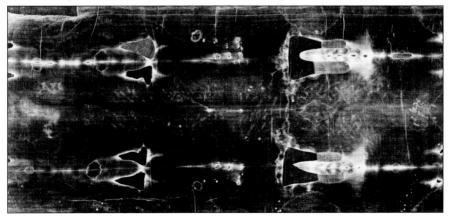

But there was more. Barbet had come to understand something that was even more telling than the details of the individual scourge marks. His interpretation of the location of these scourge marks on the body image caught my attention. After reading his description, I was easily able to confirm their position. The stripes on the back image are oblique, slanting upward toward the right and left shoulders (figures 3.4, 3.5). On the buttocks, they change position and are no longer oblique; they are horizontal. On the legs, they are again oblique, slanting downward toward the left. Like Barbet, I contemplated these scourge marks, and I envisioned two floggers, one on each side, standing slightly behind the victim.[3] They would have alternately flogged their victim at shoulder height, causing the oblique stripes of the back. Then they would have struck at waist level, causing the horizontal stripes of the lower backside. Finally, the soldiers would have taken downward swings toward the legs, causing the lower oblique leg wounds. Each strike of small bones on flesh would abrade and tear the skin, and blood would flow. Later, these abrasions and torn skin would ooze clear body fluid like the scraped knees of my boyhood. These injuries would remain moist for hours and would eventually allow for the transfer of the bloody exudates from body to cloth. As one can see, there are many of these marks on the man of the shroud. These marks witness to a true scourging. This man was horribly tortured, and scourging alone was enough to have led to his death. More about this later.

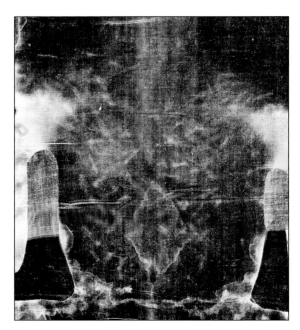

Figure 3.4: Direction of scourge marks of the back

Scourge marks of the back are oblique, slanting upward.

Figure 3.5: Direction of scourge marks of the buttocks and legs

On the buttocks, the scourge marks change position and are no longer oblique; they are horizontal. On the lower legs, they are again oblique, slanting downward toward the left.

In that Jesus was being accused of claiming to be a king, the soldiers taunted him accordingly: "And the soldiers wove a crown of thorns and put it on his head, and they dressed him in a purple robe. They kept coming up to him, saying, 'Hail, King of the Jews!' and striking him on the face" (John 19:2–3). Figures 3.6 and 3.7 show the blood marks of the frontal and occipital (back) areas of the head. These blood marks appear to be secondary to numerous puncture wounds that easily could have been caused by a crown of thorns.

Figure 3.6: Front image blood marks from a crown of thorns
The blood marks on the cloth are the mirror image of the blood marks that were on the man as seen in the black-and-white negative image.

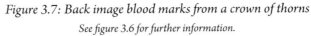

Figure 3.7: Back image blood marks from a crown of thorns
See figure 3.6 for further information.

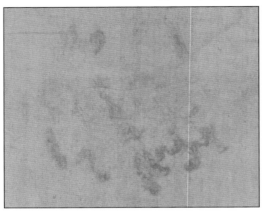
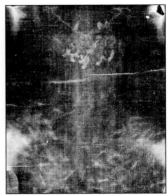

The scalp, being very vascular, has lots of blood vessels, and any wound of the head can cause much bleeding. I recall one of my first encounters with a young man who came into the emergency room with bleeding from a wound to the scalp. He was covered with blood, and on cleaning it away I expected to see a large wound. However, I was surprised to see that it was a very small, hardly visible wound, which had bled profusely. The man of the shroud, therefore, probably lost much blood from these numerous puncture wounds of the scalp.

Figure 3.8: Facial image with swelling under right eye

Facial image demonstrates a definite swelling below his right eye as compared to the smoother area below his left eye.

Besides the blood marks, on examining the image of the man's face, we find a definite swelling at the cheekbone under the right eye,[4] corresponding to John's statement that the soldiers were "striking him on the face" (John 19:3) (figure 3.8). In medicine, we are always comparing body symmetry versus asymmetry, and this facial image demonstrates a definite swelling below his right eye as compared to the smoother area below his left eye. This swelling, defined as a contusion, was likely caused by a fist or stick striking the face. There are other swellings of the face that are less obvious.

"Pilate asked them, 'Shall I crucify your King?' The chief priests answered, 'We have no king but the emperor.' Then he handed him over to them to be crucified" (John 19:15–16). In John's Gospel, it is Thomas who tells us that Jesus was nailed to the cross. "Unless I see the mark of the nails in his hands, and put my finger in the mark of the nails and my hand in his side, I will not believe" (John 20:25). Figures 3.9 and 3.10 show the blood marks of the wrist and foot of the man of the shroud. The sole of this foot can be seen as an imprint in blood.

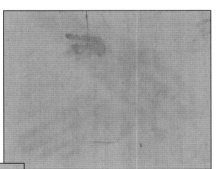

Figure 3.9: Nail wound of the left wrist of the man of the shroud

Each hand has four fingers and no thumb. Remember, the cloth was laid on the body, and the cloth's image and blood marks are in the reversed position of the blood and man that were covered by the cloth.

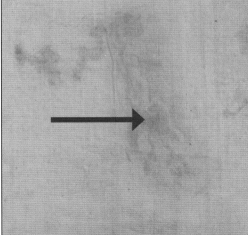

Figure 3.10: Sole of the right foot outlined in blood (heel up, toes down)

Note the blood marks to the left of the heel — blood flow from the open nail wound.

Regarding the nail wound of the wrist, Barbet's study gave a very insightful description of this wound. Barbet reasoned that the blood flow from the wound at the wrist flowed straight down, "following the law of gravity."[5] From the vertical flow of this blood mark, he calculated the position of the forearm to be 65 degrees from the vertical. In more simple terms, the graphics of this blood mark confirm that the forearm of the man of the shroud had previously been in the position of crucifixion (figure 3.11). Even after these many years, I marvel at Barbet's description; he was the first to forensically confirm that the man of the shroud was definitely crucified. Barbet was my mentor in many ways. His work was certainly one of the reasons that encouraged me to eventually pursue my own study of the shroud.

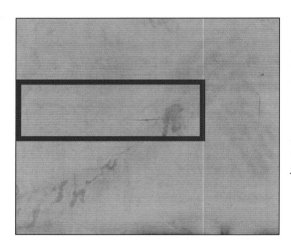

Figure 3.11: Blood mark confirming that the forearm of the man of the shroud was in the position of crucifixion

The blue rectangle simulates a crossbeam. Note how the blood at the wound of the wrist flows down, following the force of gravity.

For centuries, people believed that those crucified had nails placed through the palms of their hands when being secured to the cross. Prior to the fifteenth and sixteenth centuries, almost all art forms placed the nails through the palms of the hands.[6] Using cadavers, Barbet demonstrated that the nails had to be placed through the bony and ligamentous structures of the wrist to hold the weight of a body in the position of crucifixion. When the nail was placed in the palm of the hand, the nail would tear through the flesh and not be able to hold up the weight of the body. Therefore, the shroud image, with its wrist wound, is anatomically correct.[7]

Intrigued by the wrist wound, Barbet went on to do another experiment. In his own words, "But these experiments had yet another surprise in store for me. I have stressed the point that I was operating on hands which still had life in them immediately after the amputation of the arm. Now, I observed on the first occasion, and regularly from then onwards, that at the moment when the nail went through the soft anterior parts [of the wrist], the palm being upwards, the thumb would bend sharply and would be exactly facing the palm by the contraction of the thenar muscles, while the four fingers bent very slightly."[8] "The contraction of these thenar muscles, which were still living like their motor nerve, could easily be explained by the mechanical stimulation of the median nerve.... And that is why, on the shroud, the two hands when seen from behind only show four fingers and why the two thumbs are hidden in the palms. Could a forger have imagined this?"[9]

Look again at the hands of the shroud; note that there are no thumbs (figure 3.9). Barbet's final words on the nails through the wrists say it all: "It is useless to search for an adjective to describe the excruciating pain caused by the continuing trauma to this nerve."[10]

"So they took Jesus; and carrying the cross by himself, he went out to what is called The Place of the Skull, which in Hebrew is called Golgotha. There they crucified him, and with him two others, one on either side, with Jesus between them" (John 19:16–18). Jesus carried his own cross. Compatible with John's description of the event, Barbet noted a subtle change in the scourge marks on the right upper back of the man of the shroud that is consistent with the story of Jesus carrying his cross.[11] In figure 3.12 are the scourge marks of the back of the man of the shroud. Through the use of ultraviolet light photography, the scourge marks can be more easily visualized.[12] Looking carefully, one can see that the scourge marks extend from the lower back to the top of the back. The scourge marks of the right and left

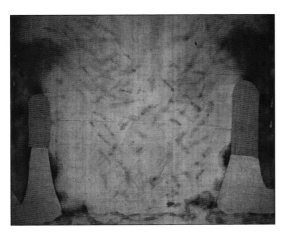

Figure 3.12: Scourge marks of the upper back widened by carrying a heavy load on the shoulders

The scourge marks of the right and left upper back are wider and broader than those scourge marks of the center and lower back. The color view of the scourge marks is better visualized here because ultraviolet (UV) light was used instead of the usual white light photography. UV light enhances the details of the scourge marks.

upper back are wider and broader than those scourge marks of the center and lower back. That widening of the scourge marks is compatible with having the weight of a heavy object pressing down over the scourge wounds of his shoulders. From this description, we can see that the man of the shroud carried a heavy weight on his shoulders, which was likely his own cross (figure 3.12).

> Since it was the day of Preparation, the Jews did not want the bodies left on the cross during the sabbath, especially because that sabbath was a day of great solemnity. So they asked Pilate to have the legs of the crucified men broken and the bodies removed. Then the soldiers came and broke the legs of the first and of the other who had been crucified with him. But when they came to Jesus and saw that he was already dead, they did not break his legs. Instead, one of the soldiers pierced his side with a spear, and at once blood and water came out. (John 19:31–34)

In the next image is the chest blood mark at the side of the man of the shroud (figure 3.13). An elliptical wound that could easily have been made by a spear is seen at the top of the blood mark. The blood flows vertically through the open chest wound, as does the blood at the wrist, another confirmation that the man of the shroud died in the upright position of crucifixion.

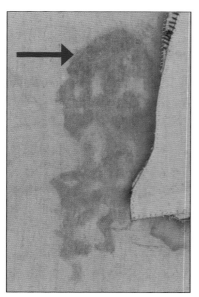

Figure 3.13: Chest wound

An elliptical wound that could easily have been made by a spear is seen at the top of the blood mark.

Note the repair patch added after the fire of 1532.

Looking at the back of the crucified man of the shroud, we can see, at the small of the back, a flow of blood (figure 3.14) that likely poured out from the open chest wound (figure 3.13) onto the linen cloth as the man of the shroud was moved from an upright crucified position to a supine burial position. On close observation of the stream of blood at the small of the back, there are light, nearly colorless areas of fluid interspersed between the darker areas of blood, reminiscent of John's words "and at once blood and water came out" (John 19:34).

Figure 3.14: A flow of blood and "water" at the small of the back

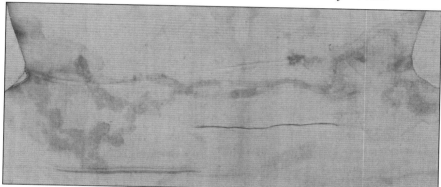

Here we have to ask why we see blood and "water" that came from the chest wound from the man of the shroud when he was moved from the vertical position of crucifixion to the supine position of burial. Is there a pathophysiological reason for this flow of blood and water to occur? Is there a perfectly sound medical reason why John would have reported that "one of the soldiers pierced his side with a spear, and at once blood and water came out"?

There is a medical reason that could explain why blood and water are seen on the shroud. First, we know that the man of the shroud had numerous blood flows that were caused by many small scalp wounds, which could have bled profusely. Second, there are many scourge marks, front and back, extending from the upper chest and back all the way down to the lower legs. All of these flesh wounds (like a serious skin burn) would cause a great deal of body fluid to go to these areas of skin injury and deplete fluid from the blood supply of the veins and arteries of the body. The combination of this loss of fluid from areas of skin injury with the loss of blood from the head and body, plus the body's physical stress of struggling to breathe in the crucified position would easily lead to a rapid heart rate and, eventually, vascular collapse. The blood pressure drops; this is referred to as shock. This drop in blood pressure would quickly lead to shocked or damaged kidneys, a damaged liver, and finally an exhausted (damaged) heart. Once the heart is weakened, congestive heart failure begins. Fluid backs up into the lungs (pulmonary edema), and the person dies for lack of oxygen. In summary, once the heart is in failure, a person drowns in his or her own watery fluids, which have backed up into the lungs.

If someone is in heart failure and a very small tube is placed down into the trachea and into a large bronchus (tube) of a lung, one would find that the fluid drawn from that area is clear fluid, which looks just like water. Therefore, if someone had just died in heart failure (fluid in the tubes of the lungs plus pleural effusion — fluid between the chest wall and lung), one would expect to see both blood and water come forth from a spear wound. That spear would have entered not only the lung but also the large vessels of the chest and possibly the heart. Such a wound would result in the flow of blood and water. So the final cause of death for the man of the shroud is very likely the same cause of death that Jesus experienced. [For more information on blood and water, see note 3.1.]

The forensic evidence of the blood marks seen on this cloth demonstrate that the body of a crucified man had been placed in the supine position on one end of the shroud and then covered by the other end of this long cloth. But most important is the visual reality of a man beaten about the face, a man "crowned by thorns," a man scourged, a man who carried his cross, a man nailed to a cross, and a man pierced by a lance that brought forth "blood and water." Remarkably, John wrote about all the details that are seen on this Turin cloth. They all correspond exactly to John's description of Jesus' torture, crucifixion, and death. In other words, all the significant wounds on the shroud are found in John's Gospel. So, what John saw on the day Jesus died is exactly what happened to the man who was buried in this Turin cloth. From a forensic perspective of the blood marks, the man of the shroud and Jesus are very likely the same person. What you see is what you get. And there is even more to see.

CHAPTER 4

◇◇◇◇◇◇◇◇◇

Forbidden Images

OTHER THAN THE blood marks, what other eyewitness evidence suggests that the shroud is part of the story of Jesus' crucifixion, death, and burial? John tells us, "When the soldiers had crucified Jesus, they took his clothes and divided them into four parts, one for each soldier" (John 19:23). Our witness is describing another detail of the Crucifixion that is compatible with what we see on the shroud, an image of a naked man. But nowhere did John mention the image of Jesus' body. There is not a word of an image. Thus, it is no wonder why a controversy has raged since the shroud first appeared in the 1350s in the West, in Lirey, France,[1] of this being the burial cloth of Jesus.

The question is, if John had seen the shroud with its bloodstained image, why did he not just say so? Incredibly, there is an answer to that question in Josephus's history of the Jews. Josephus lived from AD 37 to 100. His understanding of the Jewish world paralleled John's life as John wrote his Gospel. The following excerpt from Josephus's writings tells us something very important about the time and place where Jesus lived. The following paragraphs present a compelling reason why John would have avoided any direct statement that he saw an image on Jesus' shroud.

> Now Caius Caesar did so grossly abuse the fortune he had arrived at, as to take himself to be a god, and to desire to be so called also, and to cut off those of the greatest nobility out of his country. He also extended his impiety as far as the Jews. Accordingly, he sent Petronius with an army to Jerusalem, to place his statues in the

temple, and commanded him that, in case the Jews would not admit of them, he should slay those that opposed it, and carry all the
rest of the nation into captivity: but God concerned himself with
these his commands.[2]

Josephus goes on to relate the Jews' response:

But now the Jews got together in great numbers with their wives
and children into that plain that was by Ptolemais, and made sup-
plication to Petronius, first for their laws, and, in the next place,
for themselves. So he was prevailed upon by the multitude of the
supplicants, and by their supplications, and left his army and the
statues at Ptolemais, and then went forward into Galilee, and called
together the multitude and all the men of note to Tiberias, and
showed them the power of the Romans, and the threatenings of
Caesar; and, besides this, proved that their petition was unreason-
able, because while all the nations in subjection to them had placed
the images of Caesar in their several cities, among the rest of their
gods, for them alone to oppose it, was almost like the behaviour of
revolters, and was injurious to Caesar.[2]

Josephus further relates the Jews' strict adherence to their laws:

And when they insisted on their law, and the custom of their country,
and how it was not only not permitted them to make either an image
of God, or indeed of a man, and to put it in any despicable part of
their country, much less in the temple itself, Petronius replied, "And
am not I also," said he, "bound to keep the law of my own lord? For
if I transgress it, and spare you, it is but just that I perish; while he
that sent me, and not I, will commence a war against you; for I am
under command as well as you." Hereupon the whole multitude
cried out that they were ready to suffer for their law. Petronius then
quieted them, and said to them, "Will you then make war against
Caesar?" The Jews said, "We offer sacrifices twice every day for
Caesar, and for the Roman people"; but that if he would place the
images among them, he must first sacrifice the whole Jewish nation;
and that they were ready to expose themselves, together with their

children and wives, to be slain. At this Petronius was astonished, and pitied them, on account of the inexpressible sense of religion the men were under, and that courage of theirs which made them ready to die for it; so they were dismissed without success.[2]

Josephus's story is clear: it was "not permitted them to make either an image of God, or indeed of a man." For the Jews, images were forbidden, so forbidden that the Jews were prepared to die rather than have the image of God in their country. Moreover, Josephus was making it clear that not only was the image of God forbidden but also the image of man: "or indeed of a man." Why did the Jews forbid images in their country? The most obvious biblical answer to that question is found in Exodus. It is the second of the Ten Commandments.

You shall not make for yourself an idol, whether in the form of anything that is in heaven above, or that is on the earth beneath, or that is in the water under the earth. You shall not bow down to them or worship them; for I the Lord your God am a jealous God, punishing children for the iniquity of parents, to the third and the fourth generation of those who reject me, but showing steadfast love to the thousandth generation of those who love me and keep my commandments. (Exod. 20: 4–6)

John was a Jew and a person of his time, and he knew the Torah, which was the Jewish Law. He knew that images of man were considered objects of idolatry. He also knew the sensitivities of his Jewish countrymen, and he would have known that the image that we see on the shroud, the image "of a man," would have been sought out and destroyed if its existence had been known. Further, the Mishnah (the oral tradition of Moses) considers images in the following passage: "All images are forbidden because they are worshipped once a year."[3] In summary, John had a compelling rationale for omitting any discussion of an image on the shroud in his Gospel.

◇◇◇◇◇◇◇◇◇

CHAPTER 5

The Shroud under a Microscope

AFTER HAVING FIRST seen the Shroud of Turin in 1978, in spite of what I knew of the incredible correlation between the Gospel of John and the blood marks as well as the uniqueness of the image being an ancient negative, I was still skeptical and wanted more data. The blood marks look like real blood, but I wanted to go a step further; I was looking for a positive test for blood. And could the image have been painted? Fortunately, the answers were close at hand.

Immediately after the shroud exhibition in 1978, a group of American scientists known as the Shroud of Turin Research Project (STURP) came together to study the shroud. This team of scientists spent more than 120 hours conducting tests on the shroud. Fr. Peter Rinaldi, an Italian priest from Port Chester, New York, was their major negotiator behind the scenes. He opened the door for the American team to have access to the shroud. I was fortunate to have been in Turin at the end of the exhibition just before the study began. Fr. Peter, whom I had previously contacted, introduced me to many of the STURP scientists, some of whom have become lifelong colleagues. It was this group that delivered the hard data demonstrating that what looks like blood on the shroud is blood and providing other evidence that the image is not a painting.

It was during this 1978 International Congress on the Shroud of Turin that I was first introduced to Dr. John Jackson, a physicist, who was the energy behind the American move to study the shroud. His presentation was one of the highlights of the congress. He presented his study of having placed a photograph of the shroud image under a VP-8 image analyzer. This electronic device is "ideally suited for determining whether a given image contains distance information because it converts image shading into relief."[1] Jackson found that the image of the shroud carries three-dimensional data that is not found in a photograph.[2] This three-dimensional data intrigued a number of scientists who followed this enthusiastic man to Turin. John Jackson's drive, along with the efforts of all those who came with Jackson to Turin in 1978, deserves much credit for establishing the American scientific literature that is now available on the shroud.

Shortly thereafter, I met Vernon Miller in the grand room of the congress, and I was excited to learn that he was the official scientific photographer for the American scientific team. I had no idea where that initial meeting would eventually lead. Over the years we had a great time exchanging different ideas regarding the blood and image of the shroud; Miller was always so generous in providing me photos that I needed for my studies of the burial cloth. Years later, Miller told me that he wanted to have all his photos digitized for future generations; before his passing he gave his entire collection to another STURP member, Tom D'Muhala. From 2012 until 2019, D'Muhala and I worked on organizing and digitizing Vernon's magnificent shroud collection, which is now available worldwide at shroudphotos.com, fulfilling Miller's wish. [For more on Vernon Miller and his photographs of the Shroud of Turin, see note 5.1.]

A couple of years after my first encounter with Miller, we met again at a Boston restaurant. He had with him a folder of shroud slides. He held his hand out over the table, handing me a slide that he explained was a micrograph that was taken at 64x magnification at the image area of the nose, which happens to be the darkest portion of the entire shroud image. I held the slide to the light, and I could see the basic structure and color that was responsible for the image (figure 5.1). There was no paint causing the image; anyone could verify this by simply looking at the slide. I could see that the individual fibers of each thread were yellowed. It was these individual yellowed fibers of each thread, not paint, that caused the image.

Subsequently, Miller sent me other micrographs. One of them was taken at the blood area of the chest wound at 32x magnification (figure 5.2). In and about the threads made up of fibers is intertwined debris that was determined to be blood. Originally the blood likely covered the threads, but over time some were abraded off, resulting in less blood on the top threads but leaving the blood in between the threads. Included are two more micrographs (figures 5.3, 5.4) for comparison to the blood area. Both are taken also at 32x magnification, one at the image area of the right eye and the other at a location with no image (a no-image area). Just like the micrograph of the nose image taken at 64x magnification, no debris can be seen here.

Figure 5.1: Micrograph taken at the image area of the nose at 64x magnification

Figure 5.2: Micrograph taken at the blood area of
the chest wound at 32x magnification

With Miller's micrographs in hand, I was convinced that the image was not a painting. I wasn't alone. All of the American scientists who studied the shroud

Figure 5.3: Micrograph taken at the image area of the right eye at 32x magnification

Figure 5.4: Micrograph taken at a no-image area at 32x magnification

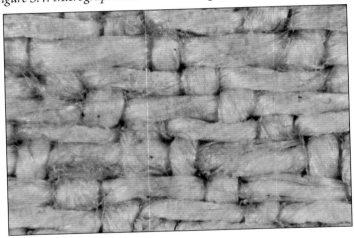

found that it was not a painting.[3,4] (The work of one scientist,[5] who believed the shroud to be a painting, was carefully reviewed by the other scientists. After careful evaluation, their conclusion was still the same: the shroud image is not a painting.[6])
However, I did not know what had caused the yellowing of the fibers, and I wanted further confirmation that what looked like blood was indeed blood.

The answers to these two questions came from a man who did not attend the congress in 1978. During the examination of 1978, sticking-tapes had been placed over the blood marks and image marks of the shroud. Some of these tapes were given to Dr. Alan Adler. Adler, a professor of chemistry from Western Connecticut State University, was an expert on porphyrins, which are organic chemicals that form part of the structure of red blood cells. Adler analyzed the particles and fibers that adhered to the sticking-tapes.

My first encounter with Alan Adler was in his office at Western Connecticut State University in 1982. As I entered his office, he was sitting at his desk surrounded by walls covered with books from floor to ceiling. We began by discussing his work on the red-orange globules that he found on the sticking-tapes that had been placed over the blood areas of the shroud. He told me of the difficulties that he had faced in removing these particles from the tapes in order to prepare them for chemical analysis. He spent a great deal of time explaining his confirmatory tests for blood.

First, he visually compared the microscopic examination of the shroud blood area to a control: a three-hundred-year-old linen saturated a year before with human blood. Under the microscope, the fibers and the crystals of both were similar in physical appearance, except the crystals of his control sample were slightly more garnet colored.[7] After this examination, he eventually "established by detection of heme derivatives, bile pigments, and proteins" the presence of whole blood on the shroud.[8] Anyone interested in pursuing the chemistry of Adler's blood studies should refer to his excellent journal articles.[9] At the time, there was no direct test, as there is now, to absolutely confirm that this blood was definitely human blood. But from the forensic study of the blood marks, it becomes obvious that the blood is of a crucified man, and therefore, we can conclude that it is indeed human blood.

As we went on to the next topic of the yellowed fibers that caused the image, Adler stopped and said, "You know, one of the best tests they did during those five days of testing in Turin was one of the simplest tests they did." he went on to explain the visual test that the team members performed. They shined a light through the cloth. As the light passed through the cloth, the blood images could easily be seen, but the body image could not be seen. What did this mean?

Adler explained that the blood marks were opaque, and because of this, they were poor transmitters of light. In contrast, that which caused the body image was not opaque and was so thin that light went right through it and did not produce an outline of the image as did the blood. This meant that the light went through the image in the same way it went through the plain cloth. He went on to further support this statement by explaining that the American scientists had removed part of the backing cloth that had been sewn onto the back of the shroud to preserve the shroud after the fire of 1532. In doing so, the scientific team discovered that the blood marks had soaked through to the back side of the shroud,[10] whereas the image marks were not seen on the back of the cloth.[11]

Adler then explained that a single thread of the shroud cloth was made up of many very small (10 to 15 microns in diameter)[12] linen fibers. The width of one of these fibers is much smaller than that of a human hair. Only the topmost fibers of the thread were yellowed. These yellowed fibers, composed of cellulose, were found only on the image side of the cloth and were responsible for the image. As he spoke, I realized that he was confirming what I had seen for myself when Vern Miller handed me one of his micrographs of the image (figure 5.1) back in a Boston restaurant.

After extensive chemical testing, Adler concluded that (1) there is no paint medium coating the image fibers and (2) there are no stains or dyes causing the image. Rather, the yellowing of the shroud image fibers was produced by a dehydrative oxidative process that affected the fiber (cellulose) structure itself and caused it to yellow. In other words, this process is a degradation of the fibers themselves and is identical to the aging of linen, causing linen to turn from white to yellow. Adler explained that light, heat, or an acid (such as sulfuric acid) can all yellow linen fibers like those found in the image area of the shroud. Therefore, it is not a painted image, but rather the result of a chemical change of the cellulose itself. (For those interested in the chemistry of the image fibers of the shroud, Adler's article is excellent.[13])

Adler went on to explain that even though he understood the chemistry of the cellulose that makes up the yellowed fibers of the image, he still did not know what event took place to cause the image. He leaned back in his chair and went on to say that with human perspiration,[14] the yellowing of the topmost fibers can be reproduced when linen is placed over the flat surfaces of a body. However, when it comes to more complex surfaces, such as the face, this contact mechanism with perspiration is not capable of causing the image seen on the shroud.[15]

Another study in 1978 revealed that the maximal optical densities of the front and back shroud images are nearly the same.[16] That means that the weight of the body likely played no role in image formation — otherwise the back image would have a greater optical density than the front image.

Many scientists have tried to reproduce the shroud image. John Jackson, for example, spent years attempting to reproduce the shroud image without success.

He investigated direct contact, diffusion, radiation from a body shape or an engraving, dabbing powder on a bas-relief, electrostatic imaging, and hot bas-relief (a rubbing image), but none reproduced the image of the shroud.[17] There is presently no known mechanism that can reproduce this body-to-cloth image transfer.[18]

Adler later shared with me another piece of information that continues to fascinate me. On removing the blood from the blood-covered fibers, Adler found that these fibers, instead of being yellow as they were at the image areas, were white. What did this mean? Because the fibers under the blood were white, it meant (1) that the blood went onto the cloth before the image marks and (2) that the blood protected the fibers from whatever caused the image to occur. Therefore, we can conclude that the blood came first and the image came later.[19]

Further insights on the shroud image fibers came from Dr. Eric Jumper (Ph.D., Gas Dynamics and Laser Physics), whom I did not meet at the congress but later met at the Turin Cathedral during a private showing of the shroud. Jumper, an engineer, spent a great deal of time studying the shroud and published several papers regarding his findings. In my opinion, his best article, "A Comprehensive Examination of the Various Stains and Images on the Shroud of Turin,"[20] is a must-read for the scientifically inclined. I called Jumper to ask him about the observations he had made concerning the image marks. He explained that his team's goal was to understand what caused the image.

On viewing the shroud image under magnification (figure 5.1), Jumper and his colleagues found no excess material around the image fibers. The only place where the fibers were cemented together was at the blood-mark areas. Furthermore, they found that only the topmost fibers of the threads of the cloth were yellowed, and it was these yellowed fibers that caused the image.

Jumper followed along the length/weave of the image fibers and found that as the yellowed uppermost fibers dipped down under other threads, they were no longer yellow but remained their original white. Likewise, as the fibers followed a normal twist of the thread, the top fibers were yellowed while the lower part of the fibers remained white. Therefore, whatever caused the image affected only the uppermost fibers, even to the point of not wicking (absorbing and conveying fluid along a fiber like the wick of an oil lamp) along the fiber as a liquid would do if it had been applied to the shroud surface.[21]

As Jumper and his associates teased at the fibers of the threads, they made another observation. Jumper remembers that after they left the examining room, they argued about whether the yellowed fibers penetrated the depth of the thread by one or two fibers. In attempting to decide what was the correct observation, they all went back to their notebooks to see what they had documented. Everyone had made the same observation: the yellowed fibers that caused the image were only one fiber deep and possibly two fibers deep in some places.[22, 23]

As I listened to Jumper, I felt that I was being taken right down into the image and fabric of the shroud. I was enjoying every moment of Jumper's firsthand observations. He was someone who had been there; he was an eyewitness. Jumper went on to say that he later looked carefully at the micrographs taken by Vern Miller and made other observations regarding the image fibers (figure 5.1). He saw that there were examples everywhere of yellowed image fibers lying side by side with white non-image fibers. He also noted that the yellowing of the individual fibers was uniform: the amount of yellowing of each fiber was a quantitative event. Each fiber that was yellowed was yellowed to the same extent as the next image fiber. In other words, there was no graduating difference in yellowness of the fibers. Rather, each fiber held almost exactly the same quantity of yellowness.

Now the question was, if every topmost fiber of yellowed threads contained the same shade of yellow, then what caused the difference in the shading of the image? Jumper explained that the difference in the shading of yellow from one area of the image to another was dependent on the number of yellowed fibers present. He made a count of them, and if one area was darker than another, that area would contain more yellowed fibers.[24] Regarding why we see the changes in shading that causes the image, Jumper's words to me best describe it: "It's like the dots of newspaper print. If you want to make an area darker, you put in more dots."

There is one thing that is certain: the image is not a painting. Jumper is convinced of this, and so is anyone who understands his detailed study of the image fibers and also understands the wicking ability of linen. The liquid medium of a paint, stain, or dye would wick along the fibers and color the fibers as they dip below the threads of the weave. Furthermore, a liquid medium would spread adjacently from fiber to fiber, and if enough is added, it would soak through to the opposite side of the cloth. If the paint were more viscous, it would collect on and between the fibers. Simply, it would not look like what is seen at the image areas but would look more like what is seen at the blood areas.

A number of years ago, I followed up on a claim that the shroud image is a painting and examined an artist's rendition. First of all, the artist's image was not even the same color as that of the shroud image; but more important, the medium had soaked through to the back side of the cloth. That experience made me realize the significance of Jumper's very specific description of the image fibers of the shroud. Those who claim that the shroud image is a painting will have to demonstrate that their reproduction matches what Jumper and his associates have described at the fiber level of the cloth. At the same time, they will have to create a negative image. The difficulty of producing the shroud image by hand is best underlined by the words that I heard Dr. Adler say many times: "For a painter to have created this image, he would have needed a paintbrush the size of a fiber which is less than half the width of a human hair."

Throughout the years, efforts have been made to better understand the shroud image at its microscopic level. Studies by Giulio Fanti, and colleagues, of the yellowed fibers of the image have revealed that whatever changed the fibers and resulted in the oxidative dehydration of the cellulose changed the cellulose of the fiber to a depth of about 200 nanometers (a nanometer is one billionth of a meter or 10^{-9} meters) thick. "Finally, at the fiber level, we confirm that the color is a chemically altered layer about 200 nm thick found at the surface of the colored fibers (the inner part remains uncolored)."[25]

In the last decade there has been much interest in the work of Paolo Di Lazzaro and his colleagues who have expertise in using lasers. By using very short and intense bursts of vacuum-ultraviolet (VUV) radiation, Di Lazzaro eventually was able to produce photochemical changes to flax fibers that are in many ways similar at the microscopic level to the yellowed image fibers of the shroud. Furthermore, he makes it clear that using ultrashort UV light pulses to create a life-sized shroud image is beyond today's technology. Di Lazzaro states that "it is not impossible that VUV radiation may have played a role in the image formation."[26, 27]

I get just as excited today, when new information about the image is discovered, as I did many years ago when I first spoke with the 1978 scientific team about the experiences they had while working on the blood and shroud image marks. These were the firsthand witnesses who came to understand by direct observation at a microscopic, biological, and chemical level the basic structures of what we see on the burial cloth. What they reported then is still true today. What looks like blood is blood, and the image is not a painting. There were two events. The blood came first and then the image. There is presently no known mechanism that can reproduce this body-to-cloth image transfer. And the wonderful thing is that one can see what is being described when looking at the photo in figure 5.1. Notice the yellow image fibers less than the diameter of the hairs on one's head laying side by side along with white fibers of clear cloth. Through his photographic expertise, Vernon Miller has given the world a visual understanding of the building blocks of the shroud image at a microscopic level. And no one has been able to reproduce this image at this microscopic level — though many have tried. [For hypotheses on image formation, see note 5.2.]

◇◇◇◇◇◇◇◇◇

Chapter 6

Buried according to the Jewish Burial Custom

FINDING THAT THE image was so unique at its microscopic level intrigued me, but at that time and even today I do not have any idea of how the image of the man of the shroud was made. Though there are many interesting hypotheses of image formation, none have actually reproduced this image. But the blood marks were something that I felt capable of addressing. Knowing that the blood marks were confirmed to be blood was a definite step forward. However, it was not answering another concern that I had: What were the circumstances that would allow neat blood marks, such as these, to be transferred from a body to cloth? I decided to go back to the basics and deal with the only logical option available: attempt to reproduce the blood marks of the shroud. If many of the blood marks were actually clots on a body transferred to cloth as Dr. Barbet proposed years ago, then there should be no problem in reproducing them. However, if I was to pursue this study correctly, I felt obligated to first go back into history and find out how the Jews buried their dead at the time of Jesus.

To my surprise, I found that the Jewish burial custom at the time of Jesus was the same as it is today: when a person dies, the body is washed prior to burial.[1, 2] Furthermore, this custom was well known, and Christian scholars had assumed for centuries that Jesus' body was washed because John tells us, "They took the body of Jesus and wrapped it with the spices in linen cloths, according to the burial custom of the Jews" (John 19:40). However, since there are numerous blood marks on the shroud cloth, it is evident that the man covered by the shroud was not washed. If Jesus had been washed according to the Jewish custom, then one would have to conclude that the Shroud of Turin is not the shroud of Jesus.

Believers in the authenticity of the shroud had a different perspective. For about eighty years since the photographic discovery of the positive image of the man, most of the books written by the proponents of the shroud stated that the body should have been washed as part of the Jewish tradition. But it was not washed because the Sabbath was imminent, and therefore, there was no time to wash the body. That is the information that I had available at the start of my study. However, when my wife Bonnie and I finished our academic pursuit of how the Jews buried their dead at the time of Jesus, I understood the real meaning of John's words "according to the burial custom of the Jews."

With the help of a good friend, I found Maurice Lamm's book *The Jewish Way in Death and Mourning*. The quotes below were key to beginning to understand exactly what John meant when he wrote, "according to the burial custom of the Jews."

> The blood that flows at the time of death may not be washed away. When there is other blood on the body that flowed during lifetime, from wounds or as a result of an operation, the washing and taharah [purification] are performed in the usual manner.
>
> Where the deceased died instantaneously through violence or accident, and his body and garments are completely spattered with blood, no washing or taharah is performed. The body is placed in the casket without the clothes being removed. Only a sheet is wrapped around it, over the clothes. The blood is part of the body and may not be separated from it in death.
>
> Where blood flows continually after death, the source of the flow is covered and not washed. The clothes which contain the blood that flowed after death are placed in the casket at the feet.[3]

Lamm's information was convincing. However, scholarship required that Bonnie and I pursue this back to the time of Jesus. It was during our search for the source of the ritual of not washing the blood of a man who dies a violent death that my perspective of Christianity and Judaism began to change. It was then that I realized that we could not pursue this subject back to the time of Jesus by pursuing Christianity's historical documents. To do this right, we had to follow the path of the Jewish faith into history.

I began with Lamm's work, which basically paraphrases the sixteenth-century Code of Jewish Law.[4] [For specific quotes from the abridged version of the sixteenth-century

Code of Jewish Law, see note 6.1.] This abridged version of the code undoubtedly demonstrates that there is an exception to the normal custom of simply washing the dead prior to burial. If death is by violence and blood flows at the time of death, the victim does not undergo the ritual of washing, but the body is simply placed in a sheet and buried. This is as true today as it was as far back as the sixteenth century; but in order to be certain that this ritual took place at the time of Jesus in the first century, we had to look further. Delving back to the time of Jesus in the New Testament brought forth no definite clues. It was only when I began to read the Pentateuch (the first five books of the Bible) that I began to get some insights regarding God's word to his people concerning blood. It was in Genesis that the first real evidence appeared: "Every moving thing that lives shall be food for you; and just as I gave you the green plants, I give you everything. Only, you shall not eat flesh with its life, that is, its blood" (Gen. 9:3–4).

Again, I came across this theme that was expanded in Leviticus (the third book of the Pentateuch):

> If anyone of the house of Israel or of the aliens who reside among
> them eats any blood, I will set my face against that person who eats
> blood, and will cut that person off from the people. For the life
> of the flesh is in the blood; and I have given it to you for making
> atonement for your lives on the altar; for, as life, it is the blood that
> makes atonement. Therefore I have said to the people of Israel: No
> person among you shall eat blood, nor shall any alien who resides
> among you eat blood. (Lev. 17:10–12)

The books of Genesis and Leviticus helped me to begin to understand why the Jews had a concern for blood. However, not eating blood was a concept totally different from not washing blood from the body of a man who died a violent death. The source of this ritual continued to elude me.

Eighteen months later I was still no closer to the source of the Code of Jewish Law regarding not washing. Finally, through the help of another close friend, I got the names of three academic rabbis. The first two leads were not helpful. I was in my office when I made the third call. I can remember my anticipation as I asked, "Do you know the source of the Jewish custom of not washing the blood from a victim who died from a violent death?"

The rabbi's response was an emphatic "Yes," and he continued talking. "Do you have Danby's English translation of the Mishnah?" I responded, "Yes." He continued, "Well, look at Nazir, 7², page 289. Also look at Oholoth, 3⁵, page 653. Read what it says about blood and mingled blood." He went on to explain that the concern was over the blood that flows at the time of death. With regard to mingled blood, not only was the timing important but the amount of blood was also important. It had to amount to a quarter-log of blood, which he defined as the contents of a small wine cup. He went on to say that this blood would be considered unclean. At the time I didn't really understand some of his terminology such as *unclean, quarter-log,* and *mingled blood.* It did not matter, for I now knew that I finally had a documented source of the non-washing ritual. As I hung up the telephone, I was amazed at his immediate recall of all this knowledge. I believe that this man knew the entire Mishnah by memory. The words of this scholarly rabbi still resound in my mind. I shall be forever grateful to him.

On arriving home that night, I went to the Mishnah. I found in the introduction a paragraph stating the Mishnah's origin. It read, "The Mishnah may be defined as a deposit of four centuries of Jewish religious and cultural activity in Palestine, beginning at some uncertain date (possibly during the earlier half of the second century BC) and ending with the close of the second century AD."⁵ It covered the period of time I was looking for — the life span of Jesus of Nazareth.

I went directly to the first passage that the rabbi had given me in Nazir. It was a list of body parts that rendered one "unclean," unclean as one would be if one touched a corpse.⁶ Confused by what I read, I decided to move on to the second quote that the rabbi had given me. As I read the words from the Mishnah, I sensed the age of their composition. The author was qualifying and quantifying and thus defining the blood of a crucified man. I suddenly sensed that these lines of text had been waiting there for centuries, waiting to be rediscovered and understood by our own generation. *[Note: It was common to have rabbis give different opinions. What is important is to understand the definition of mingled blood.]*

> What counts as 'mingled blood?' If beneath a man that was crucified, whose blood gushes out, there was found a quarter-log of blood, it is unclean; but if beneath a corpse, whose blood drips out, there was found a quarter-log of blood, this is clean. R. Judah says: It is not so, but the blood that gushes out is clean and that which drips out is unclean.
>
> Note 1. According to one view, in the intermittent dripping of the blood the uncleanness of each drop in turn is nullified by its smallness in quantity; therefore the whole quarter-log is clean.

> According to the other view the slowness of its dripping is proof
> that it issued after death, and it is therefore unclean.[7]

It took me a long time to grasp the full meaning of these words, but it was all there — the explanation of why the blood of a man who dies a violent death is buried with the body. Mingled blood is the mixture of blood that issues while a man is alive with blood that issues from the man from the moment of death. The blood that issues while a man is alive is not important, but once it mixes with blood that flows from the moment of death it becomes mingled blood. For mingled blood to be considered unclean, it had to reach a certain volume as defined in the Mishnah. For mingled blood to be considered unclean, the quantity of blood had to at least amount to "a quarter-log" of blood. A log of blood is the contents of six eggs.[8] Therefore, a quarter-log is the contents of one and a half eggs. This amount is just enough to fill a small wine cup, exactly as the rabbi had described.

However, in order to comprehend why blood is buried with the body of a man who dies a violent death, I had to understand the biblical meaning of the term *unclean*. The following quote from Numbers, the fourth book of the Pentateuch, helped me to come to that understanding: "All who touch a corpse, the body of a human being who has died, and do not purify themselves, defile the tabernacle of the Lord; such persons shall be cut off from Israel. Since water for cleansing was not dashed on them, they remain unclean; their uncleanness is still on them" (Num. 19:13).

In other words, all who touch a corpse are rendered unclean (Num. 19:13). If they do not undergo the ritual of cleansing (Num. 19:2–9, 17–19), they defile the Holy Place and are cut off from Israel. With this understanding of the biblical meaning of the word *unclean,* I began to realize why the rabbi had referenced the list of body parts in Nazir.

The rabbi's first reference had to do with the first order of uncleanness with regard to a corpse. That meant that all the parts of the body that were listed in that passage of the Mishnah rendered one unclean by all means of contact, as unclean as one would be if one had touched a corpse. In other words, touching a body part was like touching a whole corpse, and it caused one to be unclean. Included in that list of body parts that convey uncleanness was "a half-log of blood."[9] That means that if one touches the blood from a corpse, one is as unclean as if one had touched the corpse itself. Therefore, the blood as well as all the body parts must be buried with the body.

Considering a crucified man, the rabbi's second reference, *Oholoth*, was very specific. A quarter-log of mingled blood that flows from the body of a crucified person conveys uncleanness, the same uncleanness that the corpse conveys. Therefore, the mingled blood on the corpse of a crucified man must be buried with the body. The body is therefore not washed. The Code of Jewish Law makes it clear: "he should not be ritually cleansed but interred in his garments and shoes. He should be wrapped in a sheet, above his garments. That sheet is called sobeb. It is customary to scoop up the earth at the spot where he fell, and if blood happens to be there or nearby, all that earth is buried with him."[10]

What is important about mingled blood is not the blood that comes forth during life but that which comes from a man at the time of death. "For the blood lost while being alive is not to be regarded as life-blood; we are only concerned with the blood which one loses while dying, for it is likely that this was his life-blood, or it is possible that life-blood was mixed with it."[11] What is being described here is the "life-blood" of Genesis and Leviticus.

What is life-blood? I found a note in the Mishnah that defines it: "It is inferred that the blood which issues at the moment of death (which is what the Mishnah means by 'life-blood') is the blood that makes atonement."[12] In defining life-blood, the Mishnah refers to Leviticus 17:11.

After learning about mingled blood, life-blood, and God's blood covenant with the people of Israel, I then read the Gospel of John with a different perspective:

Then Pilate took Jesus and had him flogged. (John 19:1)

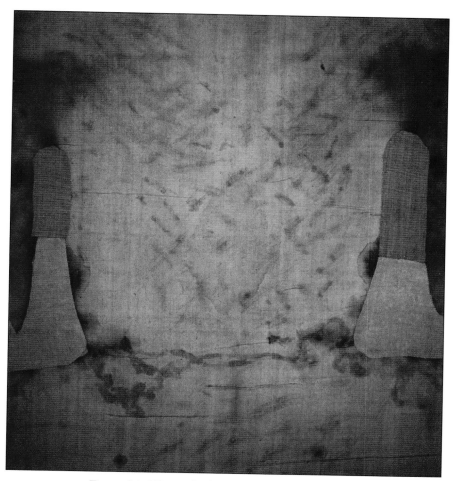

Figure 6.1: Ultraviolet-light-enhanced scourge marks

And the soldiers wove a crown of thorns and put it on his head. (John 19:2)

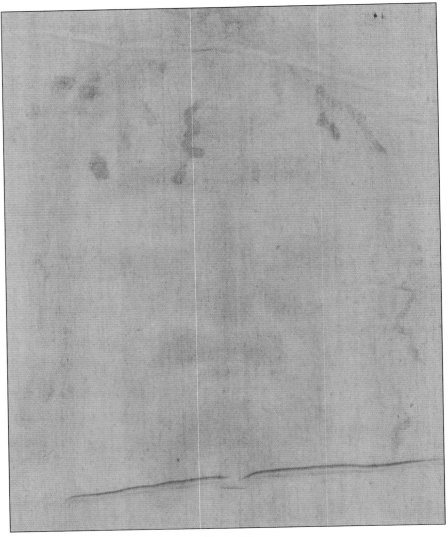

Figure 6.2

There they crucified him. (John 19:18)

Figure 6.3

Figure 6.4

But when they came to Jesus and saw that he was already dead, they did not break his legs. Instead, one of the soldiers pierced his side with a spear, and at once blood and water came out. (John 19:33–34)

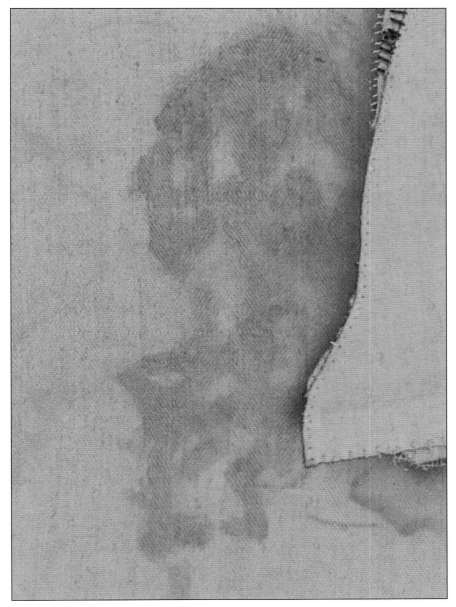

Figure 6.5

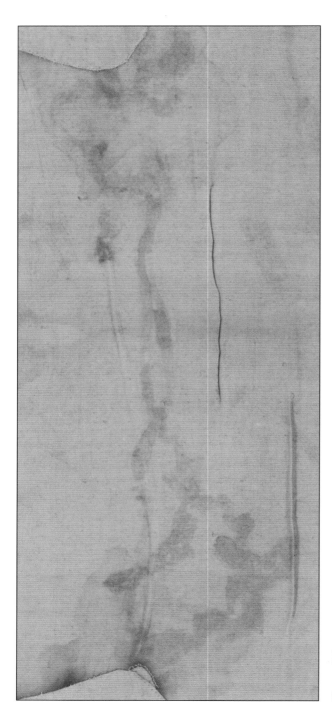

Figure 6.6

I now realize that John's description of Jesus' death had a different meaning to first-century Jews. I now understand what they understood by John's description. Jesus, who was nailed to that cross, had upon him blood that flowed during life, mixed with blood that flowed at the time of death. Mingled blood. It was life-blood, the blood that makes atonement. It was unclean and therefore had to be buried with him.

"They took the body of Jesus and wrapped it with the spices in linen cloths, according to the burial custom of the Jews" (John 19:40). Jesus was buried according to the Jewish custom. The corpse with its mingled blood was wrapped in "linen cloths" and buried. Therefore, the shroud with its blood marks is consistent with the history of how the Jews bury those who die a violent death.[13] John's description of Jesus' burial is another exact description of what is on the shroud today. As we can clearly see, the man of the shroud died a violent death that consisted of being scourged, crowned with thorns, crucified, and speared. He was simply buried in a linen cloth. He had upon him his blood that flowed during his life, mixed with the blood that flowed at the time of his death. This is mingled blood — life-blood. We are looking at his life-blood. And it is his life-blood that makes atonement.

Discovering the meaning of John's words "according to the burial custom of the Jews" (John 19:40) motivated me to move on to attempt to reproduce the blood marks of the shroud.[14]

◇◇◇◇◇◇◇◇◇

CHAPTER 7

The Transfer of Blood to Linen Cloth

NOW I KNEW what John meant to be buried according to the customs of the Jews. I realized that the shroud with its blood marks was compatible with the way Jesus' body was buried if one died a violent death. John, our witness, was again giving his reader another fact, that the shroud of Jesus carried the blood marks of his torture and crucifixion. The next question was: How did the blood marks on the body transfer onto the cloth?

After reviewing Barbet and the work that I had been doing on blood, it became clear that there are three major ways blood transfers from body to cloth.

(1) First are the scourge marks (figure 7.1) that required an "intimate cloth-body contact"[1] in order to transfer the fine details seen on the shroud. Because of Vernon Miller's use of ultraviolet photography, the exquisitely detailed scourge wounds can now be seen with the naked eye. Note in figure 7.2 the details of these scourge marks: fine scratches are now seen within the scourge marks; some of them have light areas (halos), which is serum surrounding the dark areas of blood.

During the scourging, each lash of the flagrum would abrade and tear/lacerate the skin, and blood would flow. Later, these abrasions and areas of torn skin would ooze blood and clear body fluid (serum) like the scraped knees of one's youth. These continually oozing injuries would remain moist for hours and would eventually allow for the transfer of the scourge wounds to the shroud cloth.

(2) Then there are the postmortem (after-death) blood flows that came from open wounds onto the cloth. These occurred as the body was moved from the vertical position of crucifixion to the supine position of burial. There are two

Figure 7.1: Scourge marks in pairs and dumbbell in shape

Ultraviolet-light-enhanced scourge marks, see figure 7.2

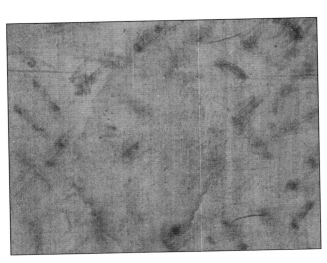

Figure 7.2: Enlargement of scourge marks of the back

Note the details of these scourge marks of the back: Fine scratches are now seen within the scourge marks, and some of them have light areas, which is serum surrounding the dark areas of blood. Ultraviolet (UV) fluorescence enhances the details of the scourge marks.

postmortem blood flows. The first was a flow of blood combined with pleural fluid (see chapter 3) that drained from the open chest wound. As he was laid out on his shroud, this postmortem blood/pleural fluid from his chest wound possibly flowed onto the cloth and continued to flow under the small of his back before soaking into the cloth (figure 7.3). See note 3.1 for another possible explanation.[2]

Figure 7.3: Postmortem blood and pleural fluid ("water") from the open chest wound is seen at the small of the back.

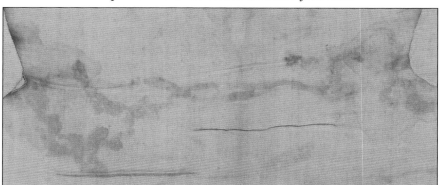

Another postmortem blood flow came from the open wound of the right foot (figure 7.4). As Barbet noted: "One part ... flowed beyond the feet into the folds, ... forming symmetrical images."[3] For each of these postmortem blood flows to have flowed onto the cloth and not onto the ground suggests that the shroud cloth was prepared to receive the body in a location close to the cross.

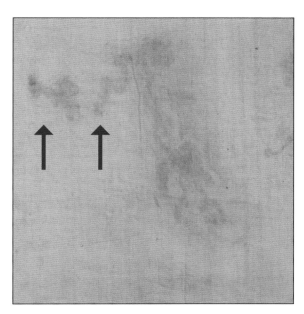

Figure 7.4: Sole of the right foot outlined in blood (heel up, toes down)

Note the blood marks to the left of the heel — possibly a postmortem blood flow from the open nail wound.

(3) Finally, there are the blood flows on skin that developed into moist blood clots. These moist blood clots transferred their mirror images to the shroud cloth by contact — the moist blood clots soaked into the fabric of the cloth.

All of these blood flows on skin have something in common. These blood flows came from deep open wounds and likely bled slowly and continuously during the entire period of crucifixion. They include the numerous puncture wounds of the head (figure 7.5) and the nail wounds of the wrists (figure 7.6) and feet (figure 7.4). Finally, there is the spear wound to the chest (figure 7.7).[4] To proceed further, we need to have a good understanding of blood clots on skin. Then we need to explore how blood clots on skin transfer to cloth.

Figure 7.5: Front image: blood marks from numerous puncture wounds of the head

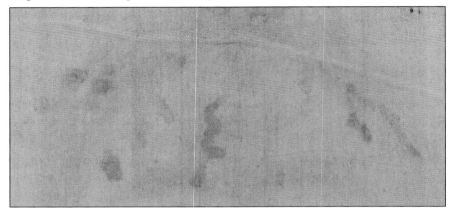

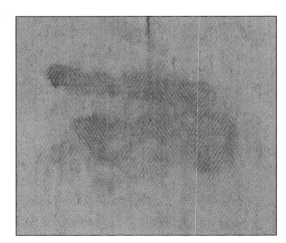

Figure 7.6: Nail wound of the left wrist of the man of the shroud

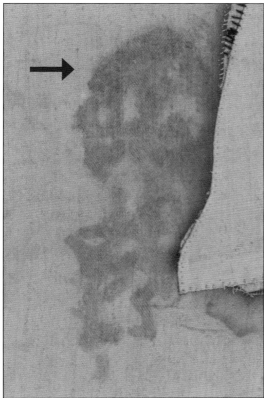

Figure 7.7: Chest wound

An elliptical wound that could easily have been made by a spear is seen at the top of the blood mark.

What are blood clots on skin?

Clot formation is the biological reaction that blood undergoes when it leaves the body. (Clot formation also occurs inside the body, but this is not pertinent to our discussion.) Clot retraction is a biological process whereby the clot actually shrinks in size, and while it does, it exudes or squeezes out a clear yellow fluid called serum.[5] Everyone experiences bleeding and clot formation sometime during life. A trauma of some kind cuts open the skin, the wound appears, and then the blood begins to flow. Clot formation occurs when the liquid blood changes to a jellylike solid red form that no longer flows but sticks to the skin. After a period of time, the clot is formed. Clot retraction then occurs when the now jellylike mass exudes a small amount of clear yellow serum for a short period of time. Finally, the red jellylike mass dries and takes on a crusty appearance.

How do blood clots on skin transfer to cloth?

The next step was to attempt to reproduce blood marks that are similar to those seen on the shroud. This required transferring blood clots on skin to linen cloth that has a similar weave as the Shroud of Turin. In an initial attempt to show how blood clots transfer to cloth, I conceived a simple experiment.[6] First, I placed a thin transparent plastic sheet on a table. Using standard glass tubes for drawing blood, I then took fresh blood from a volunteer and immediately transferred it to the plastic surface in the form of eight small pools of blood, using about nine drops of blood to form each pool. I made oblong pools of blood using the central blood mark on the forehead of the shroud image as an example (figure 7.8).

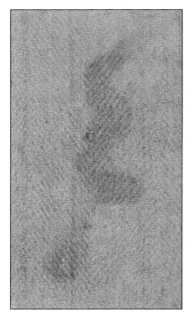

Figure 7.8: Blood mark located at the center of the forehead of the man of the shroud

Many of the blood marks on the shroud look like fairly neat blood clot transfers from body to cloth. The forehead blood mark is here to compare it with an attempt to reproduce blood marks that are similar to those seen on the shroud.

I numbered the pools of blood one through eight. I waited. It took about ten minutes for the liquid blood to clot.[7] After the clots were formed, it took a little more than thirty minutes for the eight clots to start clot retraction.[8] As the clots were getting slightly smaller, a clear yellow serum was accumulating around the clots. The clot retraction process was occurring to all eight clots at the same time. At this stage, each clot was a red jellylike oblong pool surrounded by a clear, pale yellow halo.

I had also prepared eight small squares of linen cloth to place over these eight blood clots. Exactly thirty minutes from the time that the blood was withdrawn from the volunteer, I covered the first clot with cloth. I covered the second clot thirty minutes later and so on until I had covered each clot in sequential order at half-hour intervals. Four hours from the time that I had drawn the blood, I covered the last clot with a linen square. Twenty-four hours later, I lifted the squares of linen from the plastic surface. A hard, crusted, dry clot covered each cloth. I took a penny and scraped off the excess crusted blood. I learned from this experience that once the blood clot soaks into the cloth and dries, it maintains its shape and is not distorted even after being scraped with a penny. When I compared the bloodstained cloths to the forehead clot of the shroud, I was both amazed and disappointed at what I saw (figure 7.9).

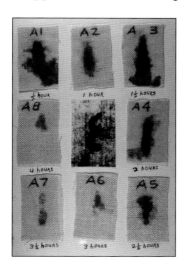

Figure 7.9: First experiment: Transfer results of blood clots that were in the <u>horizontal</u> position

A linen cloth was placed on a clot at half-hour intervals over a period of four hours. Neat transfers from blood clots to cloth were not observed in this first experiment when blood clots were in the <u>horizontal</u> position.

As I looked at the outcome of this simple experiment, I could see that the results of the transfers from clots to cloth were not as neat as the blood mark of the forehead. The forehead clot on the shroud shows a barely visible serum line (thin lighter area) around the lower edge of the clot, but overall, it was more precise (neat) than the clot transfers of the experiment. I just sat there at the table looking at the results, wondering why the discrepancy, when suddenly, in the middle of another thought, I realized that I had made a mistake in the design of the experiment. The flaw was that in my experiment, the blood clotted on a horizontal surface of a table. The horizontal position allowed the exuded serum to accumulate around the clots and cause an uneven transfer to cloth. But the man of the shroud did not die in the horizontal (supine) position. Rather, he died in the vertical (upright) position of crucifixion, and the blood clotted on his skin while he was still in this position.

I could hardly wait to start the experiment over again. This time, within the first thirty minutes after blood withdrawal and before clot retraction, I moved the eight clots from a horizontal position to a vertical position. This was time enough to allow for clot formation. As a result, the clots kept their shape and clung to the vertical plastic surface. After a short time, clot retraction began to occur, and the clear yellow serum was being exuded from the clots. I watched in amazement as the serum, following the force of gravity, dripped down the vertical wall of clear plastic, leaving behind neat, moist, red, jellylike clots. At the same time that I placed the clots in the vertical position, I also placed a linen cloth on the first clot. I continued doing this at half-hour intervals until all eight clots were covered, just as I had done with the first experiment. However, the clots no longer collected the pools of excess serum around them as they had in the previous study. After twenty-four hours, I turned the cloths over and found dry, crusted clots (figure 7.10). I removed the crusts as I did before. These clot transfers were neat (figure 7.11) and were more like the forehead clot (figure 7.8). I could now see a possible reason why many of the blood clot transfers to cloth were so neat on the shroud. Possibly part of the reason had to do with the vertical position of crucifixion.

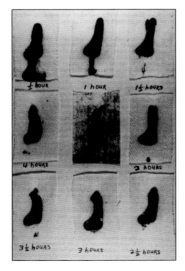

Figure 7.10: Second experiment: Transfer of clots that were in the <u>vertical</u> position

A linen cloth was placed on a clot at half-hour intervals over a period of four hours. A crusty, dried clot was seen on each cloth sample after twenty-four hours of drying.

A penny was used to scrape off the excess crusted blood. The results are seen in figure 7.11.

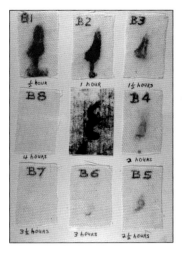

Figure 7.11: Transfer results of scraped clots from figure 7.10 that were in the vertical position

Neat transfers from blood clots to cloth were observed in this second experiment. The clot-to-cloth transfers faded out after an hour and a half due to continued clot drying.

As I watched the clot-to-cloth transfers take place, it became obvious that it was the moisture of the remaining clot serum that allowed the transfers to take place. As soon as a cloth was placed over a clot, I would first see the clear yellow serum pass through the cloth, giving it a wet appearance. This was quickly followed by the red blood cells of the clot that gave it its final red appearance as the soak-through came to its completion. Clot-to-cloth transfer occurred within a short time of placing the linen cloth on the moist clot. Once the serum moisture from the clot soaks into the cloth, the ability of a clot-to-cloth transfer barely exists, for a transfer needs moisture to occur. This is likely the reason why there are rare extraneous smudges noted on the shroud cloth. [For more on the importance of moisture on clot-to-cloth transfer, see note 7.1.]

In summary, in the case of the man of the shroud, some of the excess serum may have dripped away from the clots while the body was in the upright (vertical) position. What remained on the skin were neat-appearing clots still moistened by the remaining serum. It was the remaining moist serum that enabled the clots to quickly seep into the shroud cloth at the time he was laid out in his burial cloth. I could see from the second experiments on the vertical clots that there was a time limit on the ability of the clots to transfer to cloth (figure 7.11).

Inside, at room temperature, transfers could take place up to one and a half hours after the blood was taken from the volunteer. Over time, as the moisture continued to evaporate from the clot, the clot eventually dried, losing its ability to transfer to cloth. If, however, the clots are moistened with normal saline, this time can be extended (figure 7.12). I placed three drops of normal saline on all of the clots fifteen minutes prior to each of the half-hour sample times throughout the four-hour period. Once the cloth was placed on a clot, no further saline was placed on that clot. Overall, the placement of normal saline prolonged the transfer of neat clots to cloth from one and a half to two and a half hours. Even though normal saline continued to be placed on the remaining clots during hours three and four, one can see that in the last hour and a half of the experiment, the clot transfers began to fade due to continued clot drying (figure 7.12). Therefore, the presence of the clot's natural serum moisture is important to obtaining the neat clot-to-cloth transfers that are seen on the shroud.

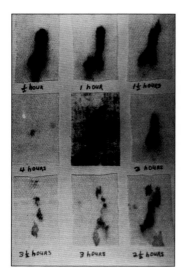

Figure 7.12: Blood clots moistened by normal saline

The experiment of figure 7.11 was repeated here, but normal saline was intermittently added to the clots. By doing so, the time of neat blood clot transfer from clot to cloth was extended to up to two and a half hours, but after that, clot transfers began to fade because of continued clot drying.

I then did another similar, normal saline experiment on the skin of my volunteer instead of plastic. This experiment was shorter, and the results were different. In this case, three pools of blood were placed on the skin of a healthy person instead of the eight used on plastic. When the blood clotted, the clots on skin were moved into the vertical position. Figure 7.13 shows the clot transfers to cloth produced by the moist clots on skin. Clot transfer was good in the first hour, but after that time much of the clot was not transferred to the cloth. Compared to the time of clot-to-cloth transfer on plastic, the time of clot-to-cloth transfer on normal skin was much shorter. I also noted that hardly any serum drained from the clots on skin in the vertical position. The reason for the shortened transfer time is that normal skin temperature hastens serum drying and thus shortens clot-to-cloth transfer time. However, in the case of a crucified man who has lost a lot of blood, it is possible that the skin temperature was below normal and cold and wet, secondary to shock.[9] Such circumstances would have likely extended the time of clot-to-cloth transfer.

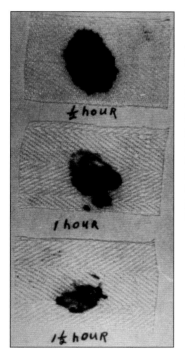

Figure 7.13: Clots on skin: Transfer results over one and a half hours

Normal saline was added per the experiment. In this case the blood was placed on the normal skin of a volunteer. When the blood clotted, the clots on skin were moved into the vertical position. Linen cloths were applied to each moist blood clot at half-hour intervals. Neat clot-to-cloth transfers occurred up to one hour at most. However, this was normal warm skin. For a man who would be in the crucified position and likely in shock, the skin would be cold and moist, which would likely prolong the time of transfer of the moist blood clot from body to cloth.

The experiment of clot transfer to cloth, performed on a plastic surface and normal skin, was not intended to duplicate the actual event but was done so that this event could be better understood. While doing these experiments, I realized that the ability of the moist clot to transfer to cloth could be affected by many factors, such as temperature, humidity, movement of ambient air, skin moisture, and skin temperature. Regarding the man of the shroud, these are all unknown factors. Furthermore, the period of time between the death of the crucified man and the wrapping of his body for burial is unknown. Regardless of all these unknowns, I learned that from the time of the victim's death on the cross to the time when he was laid out supine in his shroud, there was a period of possibly one to two and a half hours whereby very neat clot-to-cloth transfers could have occurred. What confirms this is that the experimental clot transfers seen in figures 7.11, 7.12, and 7.13 demonstrate that clot-to-cloth transfers are possible and are similar to the blood marks found on the shroud.

What is even more amazing about this timetable is that it corresponds to the Gospel account of Jesus' death and burial. The time of death was "three in the afternoon" (Luke 23:44). His burial took place thereafter: "Then he [Joseph] took it [the body] down, wrapped it in a linen cloth, and laid it in a rock-hewn tomb.... It was the day of Preparation, and the sabbath was beginning" (Luke 23:53–54). The time of burial had to take place before the Sabbath because, according to the Mishnah, no part of the body may be moved on the Sabbath.[10] The beginning of the Sabbath was between 5:00 and 6:00 p.m. (March and April Sabbath times in Jerusalem).[11]

As mentioned earlier, having worked in a hospital emergency room, I have had many personal encounters with bleeding patients. A head-wound patient can be covered with blood even when the head wound is very small. After examining the numerous blood flows on the head and the face of the man of the shroud, I concluded that he must have been completely covered with blood. This blood eventually dried and, therefore, made no transfer to cloth. The only blood clots that transferred to the shroud were those that contained moisture. Those blood clots would have resulted from the last blood flows that occurred near and at the time of death. Therefore, the blood clot transfers that we see on the shroud are what the Mishnah defines as mingled blood.[12]

In his book, Barbet mentions that he believed that while the body was wrapped, it was somewhat bathed in the watery/damp atmosphere of the tomb, causing the dry clots on the skin to be damp once more.[13] For a good mirror image transfer to take place, clots must be transferred to cloth while they are still moist. It is important to note that after the clots dry, there is no evidence of a satisfactory transfer to cloth even with additional moisture added (figure 7.12).

Retrospectively, I can understand why Barbet surmised that the clots were dried and remoistened in the cave. He would have known that moist clots were fragile and could easily be disturbed when moving a body down from a crucified position. He also saw that there was little evidence of disturbed clots on the shroud.

What Barbet did not realize was that the blood on the shroud is mingled blood. Because there is no major evidence that the blood marks of the shroud were disturbed, I believe that it is reasonable to make the following assumption: the work of moving the man from the crucified position to the shroud was done by people who took great care not to disturb the moist blood clots that covered the body of this man. Historically, the only people who would make such an effort are the people of Israel. Therefore, these efforts suggest that this was a Jewish burial.

In summary, as I did this study, along with the study of the Jewish burial customs, I learned several things about the blood marks of the shroud: (1) I was able to confirm that blood clot transfers to cloth are mirror images of themselves. That is exactly what Barbet had observed as he examined the shroud many years ago. (2) The neatness of some of the blood clot transfers may have been related to the fact that the man of the shroud died in the upright position. The presence of the clot's natural serum moisture is important to obtaining the neat clot-to-cloth transfers that are seen on the shroud. (3) The ability of clots to transfer to cloth at room temperature ranges from one hour to two and a half hours; the period of transfer time depends on available clot moisture as well as added moisture. These times coincide closely with the Gospel timetable of the death and burial of Jesus. (4) The undisturbed clot transfers seen on the shroud cloth suggest that this was a Jewish burial. (5) The man of the shroud, who was nailed to a cross, had upon him blood that flowed during life, mixed with blood that flowed at the time of death. This mixing of blood is called mingled blood; it is life-blood, the blood that makes atonement. Today, this is what we see on the shroud. [For more on blood clots and serum, see note 7.2.]

CHAPTER 8

◇◇◇◇◇◇◇◇◇

Reconfirming That the Man of the Shroud Died in a Crucified Position

THE BLOOD FLOW on the wrist observed by the surgeon Barbet many years ago confirmed that the man of the shroud died in the position of crucifixion. Now we will investigate another blood mark that not only further verifies that the man of the shroud was in the position of crucifixion, but also gives us more information about the shroud and its image. It all started with an off-the-body-image blood mark located at the left elbow that intrigued me from the start (figure 8.1).

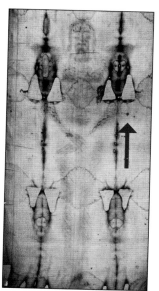

Figure 8.1: Off-the-body-image blood mark located at the left elbow

Note the off-image blood mark is at the right elbow of the man covered by this cloth (mirror image).

I did not have an explanation as to how this blood mark got to its off-image position. Barbet had never mentioned it, and I had never come across any information about it. Looking for answers, I went to the oldest authority I knew — Fr. Peter Rinaldi. He also was unaware of any existing explanation regarding the origin of this off-image blood mark.

The urge to understand the off-image blood mark caused me to consider several ideas regarding its origin, but none could be verified. Finally, one Saturday morning, I again retrieved my full-size shroud images from my front closet. As I stood there, looking down at the off-image blood mark (figure 8.2), I wondered what would happen if I placed the cloth over my own body. Would it give me more information? The next moment, I was down on the rug with the frontal image over me. Once I was satisfied with the alignment of image to body, I looked over to see where the off-image blood mark was draping against my body. The location of the drape surprised me. The off-image blood mark was touching the back of my upper arm. I could hardly believe the logical interpretation of what I was seeing.

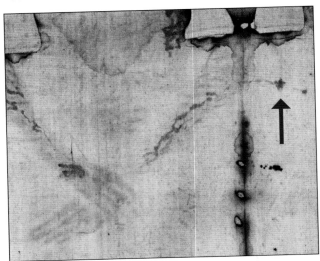

Figure 8.2: The off-image blood mark

Note that the uninterrupted off-image blood mark ends in a small pool of blood.

That same week, I began working on a full-size tracing of the left arm off-image blood mark (figure 8.3). In going through the process of making the tracing, I followed the blood line from the forearm to where it ends its course at the off-image round blood mark. Never once is the continuity of this line broken. Once the tracing was completed, I then turned it over and laid it over a volunteer in the same way that I felt the shroud cloth had been laid upon a body (figure 8.4). From this direct frontal view of the volunteer, I noted that the off-image blood mark was not visible. What I saw through my camera was similar to what I saw on the shroud: an image with no sides. The shroud image is, therefore, similar to a direct frontal photograph of a man.

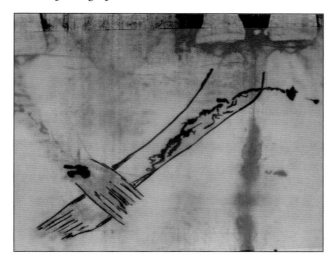

Figure 8.3: Full-size tracing of the off-image blood mark

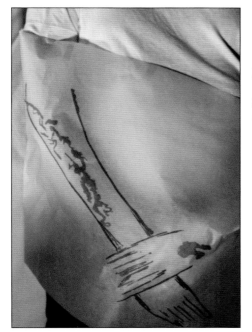

Figure 8.4: Tracing laid over a man

From this direct frontal view of the man, the off-image blood mark is not visible.

On the side view of the same subject (figure 8.5), the paper tracing drapes over the side of the body, simulating a cloth drape. From this information, it becomes obvious that the off-image blood mark was caused by the cloth touching the clot on the back of the upper arm as the cloth draped over the side of the body. At this point in the study, I realized that the other blood marks on the image translate into two-dimensional information, corresponding to the man's height and width. However, the off-image blood mark is graphic evidence pointing to yet a third dimension — depth. It was evidence that a three-dimensional figure had been under this cloth.

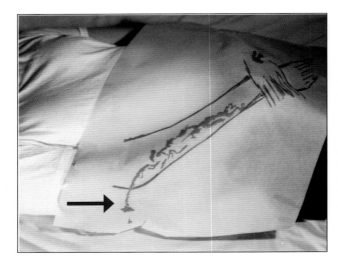

Figure 8.5: Side view of the tracing

The off-image blood mark was a contact process. The cloth came in contact with the moist blood clot on the back of the upper arm as the cloth was draped over the side of the body.

Finally, we placed the tracing and the arm of the volunteer in the crucifixion position (figure 8.6). It was then that the last piece of the puzzle became obvious. The line of clotted blood on the forearm represents a prior blood flow that followed the force of gravity. The origin of the blood flow started at the wrist wound and flowed down an almost-vertical forearm and around the back of the upper arm. It collected into a round pool of blood on the underside of the arm.

From this pool of blood, I could imagine that excess blood dripped off the body onto the ground. It reminded me of the description found in the Mishnah of the blood coming from a crucified man: "But if beneath a corpse [of a crucified man], whose blood drips out."[1] Indeed, this blood mark is consistent with what was seen at a crucifixion. Furthermore, the path that this blood flow took is real, as real as it is to me every morning after I wet my hand and razor and, with forearm

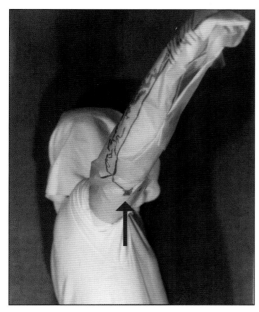

Figure 8.6: Tracing of a man in the crucified position

The blood flow originated at the wrist wound. The blood then flowed down a near-vertical forearm and around the back of the upper arm. It collected into a round pool of blood on the underside of the upper arm.

vertical, place the razor to my face and begin to shave. It is as real as it would be to any of us who have experienced holding up wet hands (forearms vertical) while waiting for someone to hand us a towel. In conclusion, the off-image blood mark and the wrist blood mark both indicate that the man of the shroud died in the position of crucifixion.

The key to this whole study is gravity. The blood had simply followed the pull of gravity, creating an unbroken line that ended in a small, suspended pool of blood. The man was later taken from the vertical position of crucifixion and placed supine on one end of the long shroud cloth, the other end then draped over the body. Again, gravity caused the side of the cloth to simply drape over the side of the victim, allowing the cloth to come into contact with the blood mark on the back of the upper arm. At that point, the shroud cloth touched the moist clot, which was simply soaked up into the fabric, leaving its imprint. This blood mark was the result of a simple contact process.

Once I understood the process of how the off-image blood mark was formed, I began to appreciate the difference between the natural formation of the blood marks and the creation of the image: (1) The off-image blood mark confirmed that the cloth came in contact with the back of the upper arm. (2) The blood marks of the forearm also confirmed that the cloth had come in contact with the forearm. Therefore, the cloth had contact with the skin on the back of the upper arm as well as the forearm.

There is a major difference, however, between the two. Where the cloth touched the forearm, the image of the forearm can be seen, but where the cloth touched the back of the upper arm, there is no image. Therefore, image creation had nothing to do with the cloth touching skin or sweat products. Why do I say this? Because there is no image on the cloth where the back of the upper arm came in contact with the cloth (figures 8.1, 8.2). Then what caused the image? I did not know. All I knew was that in contrast to the blood marks, the body image was not created by a contact process. If it had been, an image of the upper arm would be seen extending out as far as the off-image blood mark.

In summary, this off-image blood mark told me four things about the shroud: (1) The shroud cloth had covered the three-dimensional supine figure of a cruci-fied man. (2) The blood marks were made by a contact process.[2] (3) The image was not made by a contact process.[3] (4) The man of the shroud died in a crucified position. As we shall see here and later, this off-image blood mark continued to reveal its own story regarding the man of the shroud.

A Study on Crucifixion

In 1995, John Jackson asked me to help him do a study on crucifixion. John pro-vided both of us with an experience for which I will always be grateful. The plan was to work with two young, healthy volunteers who were willing to be placed on a cross so that we could better understand the position of the man of the shroud during crucifixion. We met in Colorado at John's shroud exhibition studio where he had set up the cross and the leather wristbands that would swivel. I asked John to also adjust the leather foot band so it would swivel as well. He agreed. From studying the photographs of the feet, the reasoning was that there was likely only one nail used to secure both feet.

All of the participants were in John's studio, and we were ready to begin. Just before starting, John and I again discussed what position the body would likely take considering both the study of the off-image blood mark and the position of the feet. As per the shroud image, the left foot was crossed over on top of the right foot as if the nail were going through both feet; our thought was that the effect would be that the volunteer's body would possibly lean over toward his right side. We anticipated that the position of the feet may also cause his arms to reflect what we see on the shroud as realized by the study of the off-image blood mark. The off-image blood mark as a continuation of the blood on the forearm indicates that the forearm was likely moved into a near vertical position. With this in mind, John said, "Well, let's do it and see what happens."

The young man was lifted onto the cross. His wrists were placed into the swivel leather straps and the feet were placed into the third swivel strap with his left foot being positioned on top of his right. The experiment then began. For a moment, the volunteer's arms stretched out in a classic crucified position while he balanced himself on the foot swivel, keeping straight up. Then it happened. His body moved with a jerk to his right. His left arm remained in the classic crucified position but literally stretched out as his body moved to his right. His right arm flexed at the elbow, creating close to a 90-degree angle and causing his forearm to come nearly straight down from the crossbar (figure 8.7). He literally fell into the position that we had predicted.

We were all stunned, and I asked him, "Why did you do that? Did you hear what we were saying about the possible position that you would end up in?"

The poor guy blurted back, "No, I can't help this. This is where I have been forced to fall."

Figure 8.7: Manikin of a crucified man (front view, position 1)

Right Forearm   **Left Forearm**   **Pushing upward with his legs**

Position 1

Note that the body is leaning to his right. His left arm is in the classic crucified position but literally stretched out because his body moved to his right. His right arm is flexed at the elbow, creating close to a 90-degree angle, causing his forearm to come nearly straight down from the crossbar. His left foot is over his right foot. He is pushing upward with his legs.

We were all awed by the fact that he had no choice but to fall into the position that we had predicted. We immediately stopped all activity and sat around, hardly saying a word for at least fifteen minutes. We all realized that what we had just witnessed in that studio was the authentic position of a crucified man, the exact reflection of what we see on the shroud.

We later confirmed that the volunteer's fall to the right depended on the fact that his left foot was on top of his right, forcing him to the right as he attempted to push himself up on the cross. He was *pushing up, using his legs (position 1)* (figure 8.7) to take some of the weight off his arms, allowing him to breathe better. When no longer able to push up, he would slump with knees bent and would *hang from his arms (position 2)* (figure 8.8). This would be the position of exhaustion or death. Doing the experiment again, we placed his right foot over the left, this time causing him to fall to his left. This experiment established the mechanics of why he had no choice as to which direction he moved. The key element in discovering the body mechanics was the foot swivel strap, which was functioning as if he had just one nail through both feet.

Figure 8.8: Manikin of a crucified man (front view, position 2)

Right Forearm   **Left Forearm**   **Hanging from his arms, knees bent**

Position 2

Note that there is no pushing up with the legs. The body is central but lower down with knees bent. The figure is mainly hanging from his arms. This would be the position of exhaustion or death. His left foot is over his right foot.

After better understanding the mechanics of crucifixion, we went on to do a few mock blood studies. For the mock blood flows, we used normal saline with red coloring and tubing brought from my clinic. We saw that several blood marks (flows) seen on the shroud matched with the mock blood flows that we did on one of the volunteers. For example, the red solution that was started from the volunteer's right wrist in position 1 subsequently flowed down his near-vertical forearm and around to the underside of his upper arm where the drips fell from the body toward the ground; the mock blood flow, starting at the wrist, followed the same pattern of flow that we saw in the study of the off-image blood mark of the shroud. Therefore, what we actively witnessed in the study of the mock blood flow was what was witnessed by those who were present centuries ago when the man of the shroud was crucified. In summary, this study further confirmed that the man of the shroud died in the position of crucifixion. [For more on mock blood flows, see note 8.1.]

◇◇◇◇◇◇◇◇◇

CHAPTER 9

Blood Marks on the Face

FOR MANY YEARS the positive image of the shroud face (figure 9.1) hung on my office wall. Almost every day I looked across my desk at that face, sometimes partially closing my eyes as I gazed at the image in wonder. During those years, I would always delight in showing any interested observer the blood marks of the face and hair, the contusion under his right eye, and the way the face would seem to follow me as I walked from one side of the room to the other.

Figure 9.1: Shroud face, positive image

Note the blood marks in the hair.

Over time, as I observed the blood on the forehead and hair, I wondered if the blood came out a little too far on either side of the face. I wondered if it was the same phenomenon seen at the off-image blood mark at the elbow. Eventually, I took the life-size picture of the shroud face from the wall and brought it home. I outlined on tracing paper the blood marks of the forehead and hair. I also traced the position of the eyes and nose. I then made a cutout of the tracing, removing the paper within the outlined blood marks, and made holes at the eyes that would be large enough to see through. I took the cutout and went to a mirror and placed the tracing paper with its cutout over my face, aligning the eyes and nose of the figure with my own. As I looked through the eye slits at the reflection of the paper that covered my face, I was stunned by what I saw. Wanting confirmation from an objective observer, I sent the cutout to Alan Adler (professor of chemistry, see chapter 5) with the following instructions: "Go to a mirror, then align and wrap the cutout on your face, and let me know what you think you are looking at."

He called back. "When I first saw your cutout, I thought that you had finally lost your mind and had started playing with paper dolls. But I decided that I'd humor you and play along. I went to the mirror to look, and I couldn't believe what I saw. The blood is not on the hair. It's on the sides of the face!" Alan came to the same conclusion as I had. It was as simple as cutting out paper dolls; this information gives us a more graphic understanding of the shroud image.

Visually reproducing this was fairly simple. All I needed was a bearded man. It was while I was taking the first picture of my volunteer as he was sitting at my dining room table that I suddenly realized I had made a mistake. I was not working with a vertical image on the shroud, but with a horizontal image of a man lying in burial. So I asked him if he would lie down (figure 9.2) so that I could retake his picture in the correct position. Using my full-size photograph of the shroud face, we had already prepared another cutout of the blood marks of the face and hair, but this time we used cloth (figure 9.3). I draped the cloth with the cutout of the blood marks over his face (figure 9.4), aligning his eyes and nose with the tracing. While the cloth was over his face, I applied paint to his skin through each blood-mark cutout. I then removed the cloth from his face. The painted blood marks demonstrated that the blood marks seen on the hair of the shroud image originally had been on the face of the man who was buried in this cloth; therefore, the moist blood clots originally had to have been on the temples and cheeks of the man who had been placed within this shroud (figure 9.5). The blood marks are consistent with a cloth that was draped and sufficiently tucked over a man's face that was covered with moist blood clots. The transfer of blood to cloth was a simple contact process.[1, 2] So now, for the first time in centuries, we saw what those who buried him originally saw.

Figure 9.2: Volunteer's face in the supine position

This photograph is the image of a man lying on his back. He is in the horizontal position of burial.

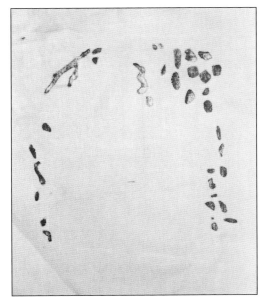

Figure 9.3: Cutout of the blood marks of the face and hair of the man of the shroud

The cutout was made from the full-size image of the shroud face.

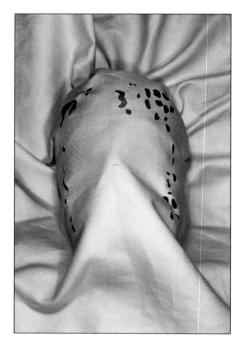

Figure 9.4: Cutout of the blood marks placed over the volunteer's face

Paint was applied to the volunteer's face through each blood-mark cutout.

Figure 9.5: Blood marks painted on the volunteer's face through the cutout
The blood marks on the hair originated from blood clots on his temples and cheeks.

These same blood marks of the face also told me something about the facial image: the shroud cloth had been in contact not only with the front of the face but also with the sides of the face (figure 9.5). Despite the contact the shroud cloth had with the temples and cheeks, no images of the sides of the face are seen (figure 9.1). If images had been produced where the shroud cloth came in contact with the sides of the face, the resulting facial image would have been markedly distorted. The cheeks and temples would have extended out to the blood marks seen in the hair, leaving a broadened, distorted face. But the nose and cheeks of the shroud are not broadened, and the face of the shroud image is not grotesque. One sees the frontal view of a normal face, the same frontal view that one would see of oneself in a mirror or photograph. What does the absence of the images of the sides of the shroud face mean? It means that the shroud image could not possibly have been formed by a cloth-to-body contact process. Then what had caused the image? I did not know, but as time passed, I began to wonder if the blood on the face and hair had even more to reveal about the image.

As I contemplated the facial image and the graphics of the blood marks, the chasm between the two grew deeper and wider until I could no longer look upon the shroud image in the same way. The key to the puzzle — a puzzle that I previously did not know existed — was the spatial relationship of the cloth to the face. I now understood that to produce the blood marks seen on the face and hair of the shroud, the shroud cloth had to be draped over a three-dimensional face that was covered by moist blood clots. I started to recognize the obvious: the temples and cheeks of the shroud image do not exhibit the blood marks that had been on the face of the man who had been covered by the shroud. Those blood marks from the face that soaked into the cloth appear visible not on the face but in the hair of the shroud image (figure 9.1). If the blood marks had been visible on the face of the shroud image during image formation, the final facial image would be more like figure 9.6 instead of figure 9.1.

Figure 9.6: Blood on the face

The blood marks on the hair originated from the moist blood clots that were on the face of the man covered by the shroud.

What seems to be a displacement of the blood marks needs an explanation. The best way to understand this situation is to summarize the events of the previous cutout experiment: a tracing of the blood marks was made that was followed by a cutout. The cutout was placed on the volunteer's face to determine where the blood marks would land. The blood marks landed on his face and not on his hair. These blood marks that were on the volunteer's temples and cheeks (figure 9.5) now lie out on the hair of the shroud image (figure 9.1). It seems as if the facial image was created not at the time of draping but at a time when the cloth was stretched out and a negative photo of the face appeared on the flattened cloth between the blood marks that had been on his temples and cheeks. This is one way to logically explain the image, but we do not know how this happened.

There are no answers explaining the above observation. The visual information at hand tells its own story. The production of the blood marks and the formation of the body image are much more than two different phenomena, each caused by a different process. They tell us something else: the formation of the blood marks and the creation of the image had to have been two separate events, separate in time and separate in space. In summary, the blood marks are a natural event, but the image formation is an event that is outside of our ordinary understanding of time and space.

◇◇◇◇◇◇◇◇◇

CHAPTER 10

The Image of an Upright Man

THE IMAGE AND the blood marks continued to reveal their own surprising visual story about the man of the shroud. The work I had done on the face accidently resulted in the discovery of something that I had never previously imagined. I had just received the photographs that I had taken of the blood marks that were on the face of my volunteer. (Remember this event occurred before digital photos were available. Negative photos accompanied the positive photos.) As I was going through them, I was looking forward to comparing the negative image of the face of my volunteer to that of the black-and-white photo of the negative image

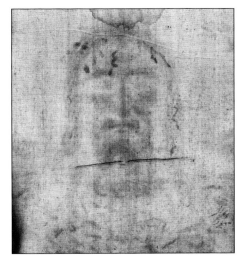

Figure 10.1: Shroud face

Black-and-white photo of the negative image of the shroud face as it is seen on the original shroud cloth.

of the shroud face as it is seen on the original shroud cloth (figure 10.1). I was anticipating a good match in that my volunteer was also a bearded man. As I held the negative of my volunteer's face (figure 10.2) up to the light, I was disappointed. His negative image was not at all similar to the negative image of the shroud face.

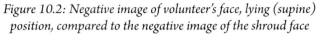

Figure 10.2: Negative image of volunteer's face, lying (supine)
position, compared to the negative image of the shroud face

 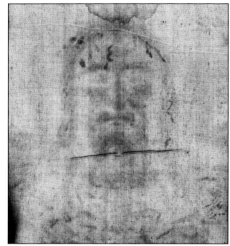

The negative image of the face on the shroud cloth shows light around the eyes, under the nose, and at the lips. The negative image of my volunteer's face, however, was a bland gray, without the striking differences of the light areas that I saw on the image of the shroud face. What went wrong? Knowing that the hidden man of the shroud was discovered through Pia's first photograph of the shroud in 1898, I made every effort to reproduce a negative that would simulate Pia's first negative. I even placed the bearded volunteer in the supine position to best imitate the image of the shroud.

Disappointed in my findings, I began to look through all my negatives until I came across another negative of my volunteer's face. In awe, I sat there. Then I stood up, and out of reverence for what I saw, I slowly backed away from the image of the shroud face that was on my living room mantel.

There was no denying it. The light areas around the eyes, between the lips, and under the nose were all there. The volunteer's face (figure 10.3) had all the same characteristics as that of the shroud face. This negative of my volunteer was photographed differently from the one taken when my volunteer was lying down. This accidental discovery was the beginning of an understanding of the shroud image that I could have never realized in two lifetimes.

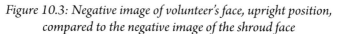

Figure 10.3: Negative image of volunteer's face, upright position, compared to the negative image of the shroud face

 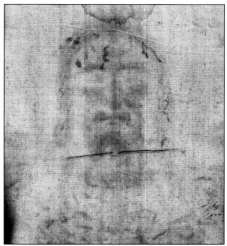

The Accidental Discovery

I had taken the photographs of my volunteer while he was lying on his back (supine position), the position that I felt best simulated the image of the man of the shroud who had indeed been laid out in the supine position as confirmed by the blood marks that accompanied the image. However, by mistake, I first took a picture of the volunteer's face while he was sitting at my dining room table. It was this negative of my volunteer's face in the upright position that best resembled the face of the shroud image. In other words, the light areas of the face of the shroud image were very similar to those light areas of my volunteer's face who was in an upright position.

I soon made a study of the negatives of my volunteer's face. After trial and error, the conclusions were simple enough, and they were easily reproducible. If light is from above, as it usually is in daily life, and a person is upright, there are shadows (light areas in the negative) around the eyes, under the nose, and at the lips (figure

10.3). If an individual is supine and the light source is from above, there are virtually no shadows (light areas in the negative) (figure 10.2).

After further observation, I found other light areas on the negative shroud
image of the cloth (figure 10.4). There are light areas under the pectoral muscles
of the chest, under the hand, and in between the fingers. All these light areas seen
on the shroud image can be reproduced. As long as light is from above and the
volunteer is upright, the light areas on the negative image of the volunteer (figure
10.4) are similar to those of the shroud — light areas can be seen under the pectoral
muscles of the chest, under the hand, and in between the fingers. Therefore, the
light areas of the negative shroud image on the original cloth are consistent with
the negative photograph of my volunteer whose photo was taken in the upright
position with light coming from above. [For more on observations, see note 10.1.]

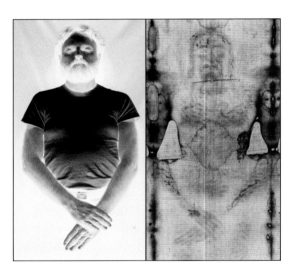

Figure 10.4: Negative
image of volunteer, upright
position, compared to the
negative image of the shroud

Light areas under the pectoral
muscles of the chest, under the
hand, and in between the fingers
of the volunteer are also seen on
the shroud image.

I then began to look further for more data that may confirm the image of an
upright man. As I looked over the frontal image of the shroud, I suddenly became
aware of the obvious. It was the hair. The hair flows down on both sides of the face
to the shoulders following the force of gravity. Looking at the back image, I could
see that the same was true. The hair flows over the shoulders and down the back
and is totally consistent with that of an upright man (figure 10.5).

To best demonstrate these findings, I compared a volunteer with long hair to
the hair flow of the shroud image. Figures 10.6 and 10.7 tell the story. They are the

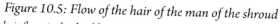

Figure 10.5: Flow of the hair of the man of the shroud

Frontal view: hair flows to the shoulders   *Rear view: hair flows to the back*

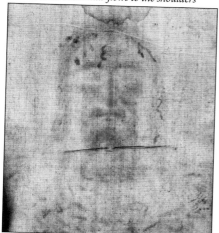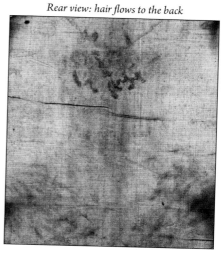

negative images of the front and back of an upright volunteer with long hair. The hair falls along the sides of the face to the shoulders and down the back. The hair of these images is consistent with that of the shroud (figures 10.6, 10.7). The next figure (figure 10.8) is the negative image of the same volunteer in the supine position. The hair falls backward rather than to the shoulders. It is simple enough. Long hair responds to gravitational force and takes on a typical appearance that is familiar to everyone. The hair of the man of the shroud is that of a man who is upright.[1]

Figure 10.6: Negative image of long hair, upright position

Volunteer: frontal view   *Man of the shroud: frontal view*

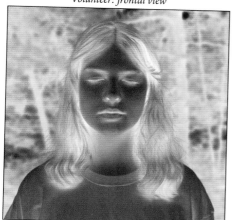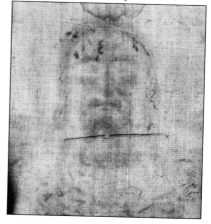

Figure 10.7: Negative image of long hair, upright position

Volunteer: rear view   Man of the shroud: rear view

 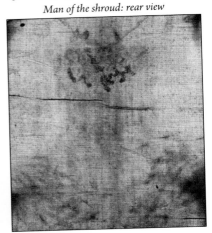

Figure 10.8: Comparing hair flow in supine position to upright position

Supine position: hair falls backward   Upright position: hair falls to the shoulders

 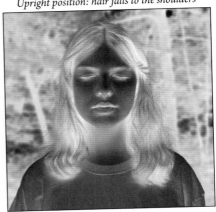

   Again, the key concept is gravity. Gravity plays a major role in determining not only how the hair falls but also how the body looks in the upright position verses the supine position. This is especially true regarding the anatomical form of the back of the body. During my years in the practice of medicine, I have been, on occasion, in the autopsy room of the hospital. As anyone would observe, the back of a supine corpse is markedly flattened due to the weight of the body; the pressure of the body weight in the supine position flattens the back, buttocks, and legs. This is also true of the living while in the supine position.

The best way to fully appreciate how gravity affects the back in the supine position is to visualize it. See the drawings (created by a professional artist) of the back of a naked man. The first drawing is the anatomical form of the back of a man who is standing (figure 10.9). The second drawing was done after the same man lay on his back (supine position) on a plate of glass with the artist looking up at him from below (figure 10.10). Note the way his hair falls backward and is flattened out on the glass. Also note the flattening of the anatomical form of his back, buttocks, and lower legs. This is what one sees in an autopsy room when turning over a corpse who has been laid out in the supine position. This same flattened anatomical form is the one that we would expect to see when looking at the back image of the man of the shroud who had also been laid out in the supine position in burial as determined by the accompanying blood marks. But that is not what we see. Rather, we see the anatomical form of a man who is in the upright position, because his form is similar to the form of the man who is standing upright (figure 10.9). Therefore, the falling hair and the anatomical form of the back of the man of the shroud (figure 10.11) is that of a man who is upright.[2] [For more on flattening of the anatomical form, see note 10.2]

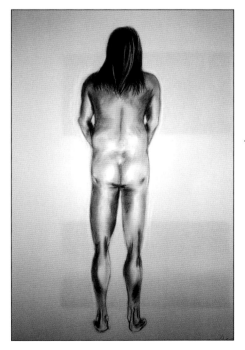

Figure 10.9: Back of a man who is standing

Hair falls to the back, and the anatomical form of the body is what is expected for a man who is standing upright.

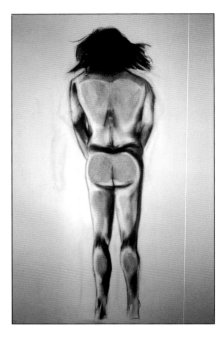

Figure 10.10: Back of a man who is supine

The man is lying in the supine position on glass. We are viewing him from below. His hair falls backward onto the glass. There are large areas of flattening of the anatomical form at the back, buttocks, and lower leg muscles. This is how the back of a person looks in an autopsy room. The weight of the body flattens the normal anatomical form.

Figure 10.11: Back shroud image compared to the man standing

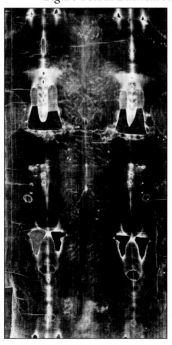

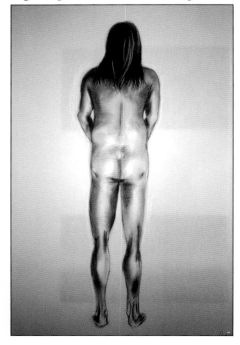

Upright, yes, but not standing. The image of the man of the shroud (Figure 10.12) shows that his left foot is on top of his right foot. His feet are crossed. He is upright but he is not in the position of standing on the ground as is the man of Figure 10.11.

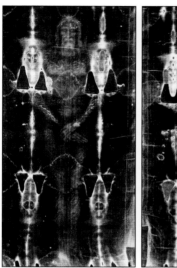 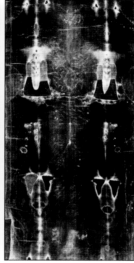

Figure 10.12: The image of an upright man whose hair falls to his shoulders and whose feet do not touch the ground

Looking at the image of the feet reminded me of an experience that occurred shortly after my return from Turin in 1978. I had just finished giving a lecture to a group of physicians on Barbet's studies of the shroud. After the lecture, one of the physicians waited until everyone else had left the room before approaching me. He was an orthopedic surgeon, well-versed in the anatomy of the body. He had a puzzled look on his face and said, "It seems as if the man is suspended in midair." I politely answered, "Yes." But I really did not comprehend what he had seen. It took me years to see what he saw that evening: the image of the man of the shroud is not lying down in burial but is upright as if suspended in midair.

Over the years, the shroud image and its blood marks further revealed their stories. Two events took place on this shroud cloth. First, the body of a crucified man was laid out in the supine position within the folds of this long cloth. The blood marks tell us that story (see chapters 7, 8 and 9). And we know that the blood marks came first because there are no image marks under the blood (see chapter 5). The second event was the formation of the image of the man. In contrast to the evidence of the blood marks, the image is not that of a man who has been laid out on his back (supine) but is that of an upright man whose hair falls to his shoulders and whose feet do not touch the ground (figure 10.12).

I must admit that I was overwhelmed with the discovery of the upright man. It caused me to back out of the room in awe and respect for what the image of the man of the shroud was visually telling me. My first thought was that indeed this image is a reflection of the moment of his resurrection. It was a moment in direct contrast from all that I previously understood. Prior to that moment, I thought there was nothing on the shroud that could visually reveal that this man's image was a reflection of his resurrection.

In the context of what I knew of Jesus' life, the image of the upright man that I now saw was a visual declaration of his resurrection. But as I calmed down from my initial moment of awe, questions were screaming inside my head: "He is upright, but why isn't he standing?" "Why is he in midair?" I had no answers and did not know where to find them. Then one source came to mind. I went to the Bible and read the four Gospels.

So began the biblical search for answers as to why the image of the shroud shows a man whose hair falls to his shoulders and whose feet do not touch the ground. I started with Mark with no success. I went to Luke and then Matthew, and there was nothing mentioning Jesus suspended in midair. I then began to read John's Gospel. When I came to chapter 12, I was amazed because there in verse 32 I found the exact description of what I saw on the shroud. And what was most astonishing was that they were Jesus' own words: "And I, when I am lifted up from the earth, will draw all people to myself" (John 12:32). It was the word *lifted* that brought forth an image of what I saw on the shroud. The flow of his hair and the appearance of what look like shadows on the face and the hands show the man of the shroud to be upright. By the position of his feet, he is upright but not standing. Isn't this the definition of a suspended man? Isn't this suspended man also a lifted man? The more I thought of it, the more reasonable it seemed. Was the suspended man of the shroud the reflection of the lifted Jesus of John 12:32? Was Jesus predicting his resurrection?

The very next verse, 33, was the comment on what Jesus had said — "He said this to indicate the kind of death he was to die" — implying that in verse 32, Jesus was talking of his crucifixion. Of course, Jesus was indeed suspended above the earth in an upright position on his cross. Jesus died in the upright position. Except for the position of his arms, the shroud image of the man very nearly reflects not just the blood marks of scourging and crucifixion but the actual position of Jesus' body, not at his burial but at his death when he was still suspended upright on the cross. But then there was the burial where his arms would have been placed on his body. These verses and these thoughts did not give me direct answers to my initial questions, but they were enough to encourage me to read on.

I looked into the writings of an author well known for his expertise and commentaries on the Gospel of John. While reading Raymond E. Brown's introduction to his commentary on the Gospel of John, I came across the following sentence: "The culmination of his [Jesus'] career is when he is lifted up toward heaven in death and resurrection to draw all men to himself (xii 32)."[3] Brown states that Jesus' claim of drawing all people to himself once he is lifted up cannot be verified in crucifixion alone. Brown says that "being lifted up" includes Jesus' being lifted in crucifixion, resurrection, and ascension. Brown also says that this moment was predicted in Isaiah: "See, my servant shall prosper; he shall be exalted and lifted up, and shall be very high" (Isa. 52:13). Brown's rationale is compelling, and those seeking further information should refer to his text.[4] Today, most of the Christian community considers that "being lifted up" in John's Gospel means to be lifted up in crucifixion, resurrection, and ascension to the Father.[5]

This whole experience encouraged me to go further. I ended up taking two years of graduate courses in biblical studies, always looking for any hints that might reveal more about the upright man. After graduate school, I continued the adventure by pursuing a long-term study of the Gospel of John. Over that time, I began to realize that indeed the image of the upright man had its own story to tell, and it was coming alive through the writings of the on-site eyewitness, John, the beloved disciple of the Gospel of John.

◇◇◇◇◇◇◇◇

CHAPTER 11

John's Tomb Narrative: What Did He See, What Did He Believe?

TO PURSUE WHAT John saw and believed when he entered the tomb of Jesus on that early morning was an exhilarating endeavor. It was part of the adventure of looking for answers to why the image of the man of the shroud is not that of a man lying supine in death but that of a man who is upright. However, there was a major difficulty. John never mentioned an image. Of course, after having come across Josephus's works (see chapter 4), I realized how impossible it would have been for John to mention the existence of an image on the shroud. Such an admission surely would have resulted in the shroud's destruction. Looking at the reality of John's time, the only logical choice he had was to never directly reveal the existence of the image.

If an image did exist on the burial linen, then how important would the burial linens have been to John? The importance of these cloths becomes apparent when reading John's narrative of their discovery:

> Early on the first day of the week, while it was still dark, Mary Magdalene came to the tomb and saw that the stone had been removed from the tomb. So she ran and went to Simon Peter and the other disciple, the one whom Jesus loved, and said to them, "They have taken the Lord out of the tomb, and we do not know where they have laid him." Then Peter and the other disciple set out and went toward the tomb. The two were running together, but the other

> disciple outran Peter and reached the tomb first. He bent down to
> look in and saw the linen wrappings lying there, but he did not go
> in. Then Simon Peter came, following him, and went into the tomb.
> He saw the linen wrappings lying there, and the cloth that had been
> on Jesus' head, not lying with the linen wrappings but rolled up in
> a place by itself. (John 20:1–7)

From this text, we know that the shroud cloth was very important to John, the
beloved disciple. Why? Because he testifies that it was seen by two witnesses, the
beloved disciple and Peter. There was a well-known Jewish law at that time: "In
your law it is written that the testimony of two witnesses is valid" (John 8:17).
Discovering John's need to be silent about an image and now discovering the fact
that two witnesses saw the burial linens opened another door for me. These two
pieces of information encouraged me to further study the text of John's story.

At the end of John's tomb narrative, he brings the reader to a very special climax
with the following words: "Then the other disciple, who reached the tomb first, also
went in, and *he saw and believed*" (John 20:8, emphasis added). Generally, the first
thought of today's reader who is already aware of Jesus' resurrection, is that when
"the other disciple" saw the empty tomb and the burial cloths, he believed that Jesus
had resurrected. Indeed, John's words create a powerful statement of conviction.

However, a careful review of what he actually said changes the perspective. On
close observation, the verbs *saw* and *believed* have no objects. What did John see,
and what did he believe? He tells us that he sees the burial cloths but never gives us
the details on what he specifically saw that caused him to believe. On further reading, I was amazed to find that the object of John's belief was not the Resurrection.
Why? Because after his exclamation of belief, John's very next statement is "for as
yet they did not understand the scripture, that he must rise from the dead" (John
20:9). In other words, he tells us that while the beloved disciple was in the tomb,
he did not know that Jesus resurrected. If he did not realize that Jesus resurrected,
then what did he believe? As I read his Gospel over and over again, the object of his
verb *believed* became more and more evident. John's exclamation of belief on that
early morning was not his belief in Jesus' resurrection. In fact, what he believed was
much more profound than resurrection. What he believed on that early morning
was that Jesus was the Messiah, the Son of God. Why do we know that? We know
because throughout his entire Gospel, John tells us exactly that this is his belief.

John tells us over and over again that Jesus is the Son of God. That Jesus is the Son of God starts with his first chapter and is a predominant theme through his entire Gospel: "No one has ever seen God. It is God the only Son, who is close to the Father's heart, who has made him known" (John 1:18). This same theme is again very explicit on the lips of John the Baptizer: "And I myself have seen and have testified that this is the Son of God" (John 1:34). Again, in John's narrative of Lazarus's death and resurrection, the theme continues: "Jesus said to her [Martha], 'I am the resurrection and the life. Those who believe in me, even though they die, will live, and everyone who lives and believes in me will never die. Do you believe this?' She said to him, 'Yes, Lord, I believe that you are the Messiah, the Son of God, the one coming into the world'" (John 11:25–27). Literally throughout the Gospel of John this same theme of who Jesus is, is verbalized several ways many times and climaxes with John concluding, "Now Jesus did many other signs in the presence of his disciples, which are not written in this book. But these are written so that you may come to believe that Jesus is the Messiah, the Son of God, and that through believing you may have life in his name" (John 20:30–31).

After the crucifixion and death of Jesus, it took an encounter with the risen Jesus for Mary Magdalene, Thomas, and the disciples to believe that Jesus was the Son of God. The question then is, why did John believe with no encounter with the resurrected Jesus? Why did he believe at the very moment that he entered the empty tomb? Mary Magdalene had already emotionally prepared John by saying, "They have taken the Lord out of the tomb" (John 20:2), so what impact could an empty tomb have had on him? What could he have seen in that tomb that caused him to conclude that Jesus is the Son of God? What was the object of his statement "he saw"? What did he see? An empty tomb, yes. The linen cloths, yes. But was this enough to instantly bring him to believe that Jesus is the Son of God, especially if he did not understand at that moment, as he stood in the tomb, that Jesus had risen from the dead? Did he see an image of Jesus on his linen shroud?

Answers to what John saw in the tomb slowly began to evolve as I continually reflected on chapter 19 of John's Gospel. In the death narrative, John tells us that the Jews wanted the bodies down from the crosses before the Sabbath. They had asked Pilate to have the legs of the crucified broken in order to hasten their deaths and thus have them removed from the crosses. Pilate granted their wish, and the legs of the two were broken. But coming to Jesus, the Roman soldiers found that he was already dead, so they did not break his legs. Instead, one of them pierced his side, and from the wound came blood and water. Immediately following his description of the dead Jesus, John then tells us: "**He** who **saw** this has testified so that you also may **believe**. His testimony is true, and he knows that he tells the truth" (John 19:35, emphasis added).

It was this quote that caused me to stop. It reminded me of John's tomb narrative: "Then the other disciple, who reached the tomb first, also went in, and **he saw** and **believed**" (John 20:8, emphasis added).

The similarity was obvious. Did John purposely elect to use the three words **he, saw**, and **believed** in both chapters? His use of similar words caused me to suspect that John might be attempting to have his readers connect these scenes in a special way. In the Jewish cultural tradition, the way to connect passages is by using some of the same words in each passage so that those who understand this concept will understand that one passage is referring to the other. This special way of connecting passages is called *gezera sava*.

The more formal definition of *gezera sava* is this: "Early Christians would have observed the coincidence [of the same words] and applied the Jewish . . . principle of *gezera sava, according to which passages in which the same words occur should be interpreted with reference to each other.*"[1]

John who was a Jew and an early Christian, would have been aware of the technique of *gezera sava*. Could John have used this technique to connect the description of Jesus' death with what John saw in the tomb?

According to John, what he saw in John 19 — the description of the dead Jesus — should also bring his reader to "believe." In the death narrative as in the tomb narrative, there is no object to the verb *believe*. Why would the visual description of the dead Jesus on the cross cause anyone to believe that Jesus is the Son of God? As I contemplated this question, another question came to mind. Is John hoping that the future reader, who has the shroud in hand with its image and blood marks, will make the connection between the death narrative and the tomb story via the Jewish principle of *gezera sava*? Is John trying to tell his reader that his description of the dead Jesus in John 19, causing his reader to "also believe," is really what he saw that caused the beloved disciple — John himself — to believe in John 20? In other words, is John hoping that his description of the dead Jesus in John 19 be later understood as the object of his verb *saw* when he entered the tomb?

To help answer the above questions, I asked yet another question. What exactly was John describing in the death narrative? It was a visual description familiar to his contemporaries who lived at a time when crucifixion was common. John was being very specific about what he saw. When John said, "But when they came to Jesus and saw that he was already dead, they did not break his legs" (John 19:33), his readers would visualize the intact body of the crucified Jesus, instead of the distorted body of a man with broken legs as was the case of the other two who were crucified with him. Here again as a firsthand witness, John was describing what he saw not only for his contemporaries but for future generations: "Instead, one of the soldiers pierced his side with a spear, and at once blood and water came out" (John 19:34). This was another specific visual detail that he alone describes; no other Gospel mentions this. As for the body position of Jesus, John is describing him while he is still on his cross: he would have been raised upright, and his hair would fall to his shoulders and his feet would not touch the ground. Does John's full description of the death scene sound familiar? Indeed, except for crossed hands, it is an accurate description of what we see on the shroud.

Even if John did see the upright image in the tomb, this still does not tell us why he would have come to the immediate conclusion that Jesus is the Son of God. When I realized that the image of the man of the shroud was the body of a crucified man who no longer was lying in the supine position of burial but was upright, I instantly perceived that this was the reflection of the Resurrection. Regarding the shroud image, that instant was my epiphany, but that was in the context of knowing that Jesus resurrected and walked the earth. However, I could not conceive that seeing this image alone would cause me to conclude that Jesus is the Son of God. So on entering the tomb, John saw the cloth lying there in the tomb. If John saw the upright image of the dead Jesus on that cloth, why would seeing that image of the upright Jesus cause John to instantly believe that Jesus is the Son of God? Furthermore, why would he come to such a profound conclusion especially knowing, at that same moment, "for as yet they did not understand the scripture, that he must rise from the dead" (John 20:9)?

I went back to reading John's Gospel, always keeping in mind the image and blood marks of the shroud. The more I read, the more I came to realize why John, on entering the tomb, would have immediately come to the conclusion that Jesus is the Son of God. The insight began when I reread John's concluding summary found near the end of his Gospel: "Now Jesus did many other signs in the presence of his disciples, which are not written in this book. But these are written so that you may come to believe that Jesus is the Messiah, the Son of God, and that through believing you may have life in his name" (John 20:30–31). The key word to concentrate on is signs. It was not only the words Jesus said, but the signs Jesus did that led John and the other disciples to come to know and understand that Jesus is the Son of God.

In chapter 2 of John's Gospel, Jesus and his disciples are in Jerusalem celebrating the Passover. While in the temple, Jesus sees many people selling cattle, sheep, and doves. After making a whip of cords, he began to drive the money changers and the cattle out of the temple, saying, "Take these things out of here! Stop making my Father's house a marketplace!" (John 2:16). "The Jews then said to him, 'What sign can you show us for doing this?' Jesus answered them, 'Destroy this temple, and in three days I will raise it up.' The Jews then said, 'This temple has been under construction for forty-six years, and will you raise it up in three days?'" (John 2:18–20). John's comment on the event was "But he was speaking of the temple of his body. After he was raised from the dead, his disciples remembered that he had said this; and they believed the scripture and the word that Jesus had spoken" (John 2:21–22).

The Jewish religious authorities had just heard Jesus speak and saw what he had done in the temple. Yes, Jesus challenged the marketing system of the temple, but most important, early in John's Gospel, Jesus publicly announced for the first time that he was the Son of God by saying, "Stop making my Father's house a marketplace!" (John 2:16). Although John does not comment on Jesus' announcement that the temple was his Father's house, it was central to the entire event in that Jesus was stating why he had the authority to do what he did in the temple. John does not mention here the seriousness of Jesus' proclamation of being the Son of God, but he does in a later chapter when Jesus made a similar statement and John commented, "For this reason the Jews were seeking all the more to kill him, because he was not only breaking the sabbath, but was also calling God his own Father, thereby making himself equal to God" (John 5:18).

In response to what Jesus did in the temple, the Jewish religious leaders asked Jesus to show them a sign. They wanted a visible sign, evidence for defending his actions and blasphemous words, words that were punishable by death. In response, Jesus then predicted the sign: "Destroy this temple, and in three days I will raise it up" (John 2:19). The Jewish leaders thought he was speaking of the temple that had been under construction for forty-six years. John's comment clarified what they misunderstood: "But he was speaking of the temple of his body" (John 2:21).

Plainly, Jesus said that the sign was that he would raise up his destroyed body in three days. That is exactly what the disciples understood, that his body would be raised up. They did not know that he would literally rise from the dead. Why do we know this? Because the beloved disciple told his readers when John himself was in the tomb, "for as yet they did not understand the scripture, that he must rise from the dead" (John 20:9). They only fully understood this sign once they saw and knew that Jesus was raised from the dead: "After he was raised from the dead, his disciples remembered that he had said this; and they believed the scripture and the word that Jesus had spoken" (John 2:22). Similar words at the end of John's tomb story (John 20:8–9) and at the end of the temple story (John 2:22) make it clear that John was intentionally connecting these stories via *gezera sava* (see definition above). The italicized/boldfaced words illustrate the similar words used to connect John's tomb story with the temple story:

> Tomb story: "And he saw and ***believed***; for as yet they did not understand the ***scripture***, that he must ***rise from the dead***" (John 20:8–9).

> Temple story: "After he was ***raised from the dead***, his disciples remembered that he had said this; and they **believed** the **scripture** and the word that Jesus had spoken" (John 2:22).

John did more than use *gezera sava* to connect the tomb narrative with the temple narrative. It has already been discussed above but is worth repeating, for it confirms without a doubt that connecting these narratives was definitely John's intent. It is the last sentence describing the tomb event that confirms his intent: "for as yet they did not understand the scripture, that he must rise from the dead" (John 20:9). Why? Because that tomb narrative fits perfectly into the temple narrative.

What is the logical sequence of events that could have brought John to connect these verses? *First*, what did he see? On entering the tomb, he could have seen on the burial cloth the image of the raised crucified body of his Lord.

Second, what did he believe? At that very moment, he could have remembered the words of Jesus, "Destroy this temple, and in three days I will raise it up" (John 2:19). He could have remembered the entire temple scene when the Jewish religious authorities demanded that Jesus show them a sign for what he did and for who he claimed to be — the Son of the Father, the Son of God. Right before his eyes could be the sign that Jesus predicted in the temple. Connecting the temple scene with the tomb scene could, therefore, give his readers the answers to what John "saw and believed."

John could have connected the verses so that one day in the future the world could come to realize what he saw as he entered the tomb. John had to have been cautious knowing that Jesus' shroud with its image could be destroyed by his countrymen if they became aware of it. So he never mentioned the image. But he prepared for the future and carefully wrote his Gospel knowing that the key piece to fully understanding the message of what he saw in the tomb was having in hand the actual shroud image of the upright man. Is this speculative drama, or is it more likely John's genius? If John did see the shroud, it was his genius to construct a subtle message that kept the shroud of Jesus safe for the future.

For John, all the events had been perfectly lined up. John had witnessed the temple scene and heard Jesus' response to the Jewish religious leaders who asked him for a sign. John had seen Jesus lifted up on the cross. He not only witnessed it but described his death in detail, which is what we see on the shroud today. He saw and described his burial. John saw the burial cloths as he entered the tomb. Then John saw the image of the "destroyed" raised body of Jesus. And he remembered that this was the sign that Jesus had predicted in the temple. It was this sign of the upright man of the shroud that brought him to immediately believe that Jesus is the Son of God (figure 11.1). If John did indeed see the shroud image, it was his epiphany — his profound moment of truth, realizing that Jesus is truly the Son of God.

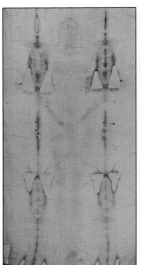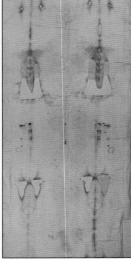

Figure 11.1: "Destroy this temple, and in three days I will raise it up" (John 2:19).

CHAPTER 12

God Is at Work

"DESTROY THIS TEMPLE, and in three days I will raise it up" (John 2:19). This is the sign that Jesus predicted in the temple. If John did indeed see this sign in the tomb, then the shroud image would have to be something very special. If the shroud image was not special, this adventure in discovery would have to come to an abrupt end. But indeed, it is special, for it is a work of God. Coming to that conclusion was a long process. *First*, we need to define from John's perspective what signs are and why they are important. *Second*, we need to explore the visible objective data that shows us that the image of the lifted man of the shroud is one of God's works.

First, what John calls signs many call miracles, but Jesus calls them works.[1] To understand what John means by signs, it is necessary to enter into the context of Jesus' life. John tells us that Jesus first spoke of his work during a feast in Jerusalem. It all began at the Sheep Gate where there was a pool with five porticoes. Jesus took notice of one of the invalids who had been there for many years. He spoke to him, "'Do you want to be made well?' The sick man answered him, 'Sir, I have no one to put me into the pool when the water is stirred up; and while I am making my way, someone else steps down ahead of me.' Jesus said to him, 'Stand up, take your mat and walk'" (John 5:6–8). At once he took up his mat and began to walk. It was a Sabbath day, the day of rest, when no Jew is allowed to work. And when the Jews in authority discovered that Jesus had broken the Sabbath, they challenged him on his work of having made the invalid well. His response was "My Father is still working, and I also am working" (John 5:17).

Through his response, Jesus immediately communicates who he is, the Son of God: "My Father is still working" (John 5:17). He then goes on to reveal that he, like the Father, is working and then gives details of their relationship regarding the works they do. "Very truly, I tell you, the Son can do nothing on his own, but only what he sees the Father doing; for whatever the Father does, the Son does likewise. The Father loves the Son and shows him all that he himself is doing; and he will show him greater works than these, so that you will be astonished. Indeed, just as the Father raises the dead and gives them life, so also the Son gives life to whomever he wishes" (John 5:19–21). Through John's witness, his readers begin to understand that Jesus' works originate from the Father. Jesus also informs the audience that beyond making this man well, there are many more works to come that will astonish them.

Jesus then goes on to give the purpose of these works. "The works that the Father has given me to complete, the very works that I am doing, testify on my behalf that the Father has sent me" (John 5:36). According to John's witness of these works, works that no one else had ever done, Jesus begins to communicate to the public and his disciples with visible signs that are not of our world of time and space. Those were works that they could see and touch. These works were testimonies of healing, creating, and so forth, objectively showing that he had been sent by the Father.

As Jesus' ministry goes on, he gradually reveals through his works and public dialogue more about who he is. And toward the end of his ministry, during the same night that he was to be taken into custody by the soldiers, we have the most complete revelation of what his works communicate.

> Philip said to him, "Lord, show us the Father, and we will be satisfied." Jesus said to him, "Have I been with you all this time, Philip, and you still do not know me? Whoever has seen me has seen the Father. How can you say, 'Show us the Father'? Do you not believe that I am in the Father and the Father is in me? The words that I say to you I do not speak on my own; but the Father who dwells in me does his works. Believe me that I am in the Father and the Father is in me; but if you do not, then believe me because of the works themselves." (John 14:8–11)

According to John's witness, Jesus' works are the visual testimony, the physical proof, that Jesus is the visual presence of God in the world.

At the end of his Gospel, John stated his final and most important message concerning these works that he calls signs. He revealed why he focused on them: "Now Jesus did many other signs in the presence of his disciples, which are not written in this book. But these are written so that you may come to believe that Jesus is the Messiah, the Son of God, and that through believing you may have life in his name" (John 20:30–31). So for John, the signs, the works of Jesus, were of utmost importance, for they were the source of belief for himself, for his generation, and for future generations.

Second, we will now explore the visible objective data that brings us to understand that the image of the upright man of the shroud is one of God's works. In doing this, we hope to resolve the following questions that come to mind. Can this image be the sign that Jesus predicted in the temple? Is this the image that the beloved disciple saw in the tomb? These answers depend on this final question: Is the image of the upright man of the shroud one of the miracles that John calls signs — one of God's works?

Understanding how to use the data that was available to answer these questions was a process that began by asking another question. What is the origin of the shroud image? The creation of the shroud image falls into three possible general *categories*. *One*, the shroud image could be made by human hands. *Two*, it could be a natural event. *Three*, it could be a supernatural event.

Category one, the shroud image could be made by human hands. This question has already been discussed in detail in chapter 5. In summary, the microscopic

Figure 12.1: Micrograph taken at the image area of the nose at 64x magnification

building blocks of the shroud image are visualized in the previous micrograph: at 64x magnification, monochromatic yellow image fibers are seen right beside white fibers of clear cloth (figure 12.1). It is these yellowed fibers that are the building blocks of the image. These image fibers are devoid of paint, and chemically there are no dyes or stains. At this microscopic level, the shroud image has never been reproduced by hand. The scientific consensus is that the image is not a work of human hands.

Category two, the shroud image could be a natural event. Serious investigations began in 1898, when the first photograph of the shroud image revealed the positive image of the man on the photographic negative plate. Investigative work centered on research related to whether the occurrence of the image from body to cloth was a natural event. A compelling argument against a natural transfer of body image to cloth is that up to this time, after more than 120 years of effort by very capable scientists, no known natural mechanism has been discovered that can produce this body-to-cloth image transfer at the microscopic level. Wrapped corpses have never been known to produce body images. This shroud image is unique in the world. Moreover, there is visual evidence revealing that image formation was not a natural event. The specific visual evidence discussed here is the off-image blood mark (figure 12.2) previously presented in chapter 8, figures 8.1 through 8.6. This blood mark, which is a natural event, also forensically demonstrates that the man of the shroud died in a crucified position.

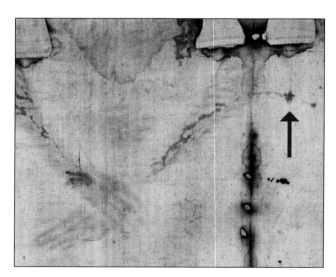

Figure 12.2:
The off-image
blood mark

As summarized in chapter 8, this off-image blood mark revealed four things about the shroud and its image: (1) The shroud cloth had covered the three-dimensional supine figure of a crucified man. (2) The blood marks were made by a contact process. (3) The image was not made by a contact process. (4) The man of the shroud died in a crucified position. Recall that the off-image blood mark was caused by the cloth touching the clot on the back of the upper arm as the cloth draped over the side of the body. The cloth was in contact with the back of the upper arm as evidenced by the blood mark, but there is no image visible there.

Natural events are ubiquitous, involving not just parts of an entity but the whole entity. If body-to-cloth image formation were a natural event, then whatever happened at the front of the arm with cloth touching skin should also have happened at the back of the upper arm since the cloth came in contact with the skin in both areas as determined by the blood marks. Yet we only see the image of the front of the arm and do not see the image of the back of the upper arm. So the event that caused the image was not ubiquitous as we expect a natural event to be. If image formation had occurred at the back of the upper arm as it did for the front of the arm, then the image would be distorted. So, in conclusion, image formation was not a natural event.

Category three, the shroud image could be a supernatural event. If the image is not made by human hands, and not a natural event, then is it a supernatural event? In order to explore this question, there is a need to define what a supernatural event is in the context of Jesus' life. In order to arrive at a definition, it is necessary to examine some miracles that John calls signs and that Jesus calls works.

Jesus' first work occurred at a wedding in Cana of Galilee that Jesus, his mother, and his disciples were attending. During the wedding feast the wine ran out, and the mother of Jesus took charge and said to Jesus, "'They have no wine.' And Jesus said to her, 'Woman, what concern is that to you and to me? My hour has not yet come'" (John 2:3–4). His mother responded by saying to the servants, "Do whatever he tells you" (John 2:5). Nearby there were six stone water jars. Jesus then said to the servants, "Fill the jars with water" (John 2:7), which they did. Then he said, "Now draw some out, and take it to the chief steward" (John 2:8). The steward tasted the water that had become wine but was not aware from where it came. He then told the bridegroom, "Everyone serves the good wine first, and then the inferior wine after the guests have become drunk. But you have kept the good wine until now" (John 2:10). This was Jesus' first sign when he "revealed his glory; and his disciples believed in him" (John 2:11).

Here we have Jesus' first work done in the presence of his disciples. They were amazed at what Jesus had done — instantly changing water into a good wine. And because of that work, they were then convinced that he was the Messiah, a prophet like Moses, but now even more than that. It was the beginning of their road to understanding who he is.

From a modern perspective, wine is loaded with carbon atoms, and water is H_2O — hydrogen and oxygen. For Jesus to have done this act, he literally, in an instant, would have had to create carbon atoms and come up with a good wine. From their perspective as first-century Jews, the only one who can create is God. So for them, this event, the creation of wine from water, was the manifestation of the power and presence of God in the world. That is what John witnessed and understood when he wrote, "Jesus did this ... and revealed his glory; and his disciples believed in him" (John 2:11). Indeed, key to understanding what John said is the word *glory*, defined as the manifestation of the power and presence of God in the world. What they witnessed and came to believe was that the power and presence of God is in Jesus. And they believed because of the work itself, which was an objective, physical event that they could see, taste, and drink. This first work of Jesus at a wedding feast was an event that cannot be understood within our world. It is an event that is outside of our ordinary understanding of *time and space*.

A later work of Jesus began when he received a message from close friends, two sisters, Mary and Martha, informing him that their brother, Lazarus, was ill. Two days later, Jesus arrived in Bethany and on approaching their home was greeted by Martha. She said to him, "Lord, if you had been here, my brother would not have died" (John 11:21). Later Jesus met her sister Mary, who was weeping and who said the very same words to him. Jesus was greatly moved and also wept. Jesus said, "Where have you laid him?" (John 11:34). They brought him to the tomb, which was a cave, and a stone was laid against it. Jesus said, "Take away the stone" (John 11:39). Martha said, "'Lord, already there is a stench because he has been dead four days.' Jesus said to her, 'Did I not tell you that if you believed, you would see the glory of God?'" (John 11:39–40). The stone was removed and Jesus, looking upward, said, "Father, I thank you for having heard me. I knew that you always hear me, but I have said this for the sake of the crowd standing here, so that they may believe that you sent me" (John 11:41–42). In a loud voice, his next words were "Lazarus, come out!" (John 11:43). The man came out.

Here John provides another work of Jesus that indeed astonishes. And Jesus does it so that those present may believe that he was sent by the Father. Here again John witnesses to the presence and the power of God as the creator. From a modern perspective, we in medicine worry about the condition of the brain if someone is without oxygen for four minutes. This man had been dead for four days and his body had a stench; it was corrupting. In the time it took Jesus to say, "Lazarus, come out," God, the creator of "all things" (John 1:3), had to re-create his entire brain to be at the very point it was before he died, plus do the same for the rest of his entire body. That, of course, is a totally impossible task. Certainly, this work can also be described as an event that is outside of our ordinary understanding of time and space.

In the context of Jesus' life and in our life today, a supernatural event is defined as an event that is outside of our ordinary understanding of time and space. That definition would also apply to other works of Jesus that John calls signs; they were physical events that everyone was able to see, hear, and touch. If they were so disposed, they would see them as being a created work, a work of glory, a *work* manifesting the power and presence of God in the world. Is this a valid definition of the event that produced the shroud image as we see it today?

It is well known that the shroud image is unique in the world and that it has never been reproduced at the microscopic level, even with the modern technology of today. But is there any visual information that we can all easily see that shows us that this shroud image is indeed the product of an event outside of our ordinary understanding of time and space, an event that also manifests the power and presence of God in the world? Yes, there are two observations that we have already discussed: *first*, the blood marks on the face (chapter 9) and, *second*, the image of the upright man (chapter 10).

First, recall the study of the blood marks on the face in chapter 9, figures 9.1 through 9.6. Did these blood marks on the hair originate from blood that was on the hair? As stated earlier, a tracing of the blood marks was made that was followed by a cutout. The cutout was placed on the volunteer's face to determine where the blood marks would land. The blood marks landed on his face and not on his hair. These blood marks that were on the man's temples and cheeks (figure 12.3) now lie out on his hair on the image (figure 12.4). It seems as if the facial image was created not at the time of draping but at a time when the cloth was stretched out and a negative image of the face appeared on the flattened cloth between the blood marks that had been on his temples and cheeks. Again, this is one way to logically explain the image, but we do not know how this happened.

Figure 12.3: Blood marks painted on the volunteer's face through the cutout
The blood marks on the hair originated from blood clots on his temples and cheeks.

Figure 12.4: Shroud face, positive image

Note the blood marks on the hair.

This forensic understanding of the blood marks on the face has produced questions that have no answers. Who or what moved the cloth? Or was it moved at all? How did the blood that was on the face move out to the hair? Who or what provided the energy to transfer the image of the face to the cloth? Asking these questions is like asking how Jesus turned water to wine. Indeed, the blood marks are a natural event, but the creation of the image was an event that is outside of our ordinary understanding of time and space.

Second, recall the study of the image of the upright man in chapter 10, figures 10.1 through 10.13. The supine position was compared to the upright position by studying the effects of gravity on the anatomy of the body. The anatomical study of the back image of the shroud shows that the shroud image is not of a man who is in the supine position but of a man who is upright. This upright position is further confirmed by the natural flow of hair down to the shoulders and down the back. Yes, the blood marks are forensically consistent with a man who was scourged and crucified, then laid out supine in his burial cloth. But in contrast, the image is that of a man who is no longer lying in burial. Rather, it is of a man whose hair falls to his shoulders and whose feet do not touch the ground, a man who is lifted up as if in midair (figure 12.5).

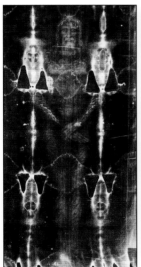

Figure 12.5: The image of an upright man whose hair falls to his shoulders and whose feet do not touch the ground

This man is lifted up as if in midair.

These anatomical observations have also produced questions that have no answers. Who raised up this man's body? How was it raised? Or was it moved at all? Where did the energy come from that produced the shroud image of the front and back of the body of this lifted man? Again, asking these questions is like asking how Jesus raised Lazarus from the dead. Indeed, the creation of the image was an event that is outside of our ordinary understanding of time and space.

These two studies — the examination of the blood marks on the face (chapter 9) and the study of the image of the upright man (chapter 10) — provide visual information we all can see that shows us that the creation of the image was an event that is outside of our ordinary understanding of time and space. The event of image formation, therefore, corresponds with what we have defined as a supernatural event. So, just as it was in the time of Jesus, when people could see the works of God, the turning of water into wine, the raising of Lazarus, so it is in our day when people can see a work of God, the image of the lifted man of the shroud. All we need to do is use our eyes and mind, to understand the objective visual reality that is being communicated to us by God.

With this evidence in hand, we can see for ourselves that the image of the lifted man of the shroud exactly fits the sign that Jesus predicted in the temple: "Destroy this temple, and in three days I will raise it up" (John 2:19). It is the image that the beloved disciple saw in the tomb. It is one of God's works. Indeed, the image of the lifted man is an event of creation, a sign, a work that we all can see today. It manifests the power and presence of God in the world. Yes, God is at work.

"Believe me that I am in the Father and the Father is in me; but if you do not, then believe me because of the works themselves" (John 14:11). When we look upon the visible image of the man of the shroud, we are looking upon the image of Jesus, "the image of the invisible God" (Col. 1:15). "Whoever has seen me has seen the Father" (John 14:9).

◇◇◇◇◇◇◇◇

CHAPTER 13

The Revelation of the Spirit

FOR ME, THIS adventure of discovery had now reached a new plateau. Right before me were forensic and anatomical observations that pointed to another world, a spiritual world. And this spiritual world is silently communicating to us via the upright image and blood of the shroud. I felt compelled to press on for more answers pertaining to the lifted man, but it became obvious that continuing with forensics as the tool of exploration would not work. I then realized that I had no place to go other than to delve even deeper into the Gospel of John. Gradually I began to discover more regarding the lifted man of the shroud.

That image of the lifted man of the shroud was the key, in that once it was placed in the context of the life of Jesus, a door was opened. The upright image revealed that it had its own designated purpose in each of the events that John witnessed so many years ago. It is the sign that Jesus predicted in the temple. It is the image that the beloved disciple saw when he entered the tomb. It *manifests* the power and presence of God in the world. It is the visible image of the invisible God. However, the lifted man of the shroud also points to an event that is central to John's witness of Jesus' life, an event that all of humanity can become aware of and choose to embrace. The lifted man of the shroud points to Jesus' revelation of the Spirit, the Holy Spirit that gives humanity eternal life.

After many years of reading John's Gospel in light of the shroud's image and blood marks, I began to understand the importance of the Spirit. John's narrative of the Spirit was not confined to one or two chapters but gradually revealed itself throughout the Gospel. It is central to the Gospel. It is the Spirit that gives eternal life. The Spirit is our gift from God who offers his Spirit as the only source of eternal life for humanity. The following is an attempt to relate Jesus' revelation of the Spirit and ultimately show that the image of the lifted man of the shroud is the visual sign of the fulfillment of this revelation.

From our previous discussion at the end of chapter 10, the lifted man of the shroud points to three events: the crucifixion, the resurrection, and the ascension of Jesus to the Father. In this chapter we will begin to come to understand that all three events must occur in order to fulfill God's plan for sending us the Spirit. It is only through the Spirit that we may indeed have life eternal with the Creator of all things. Sounds dramatic because it is, and for me, were it not for the image of the lifted man of the shroud, I never would have come to fully understand John's profound message of God's most precious gift — the Spirit, the source of eternal life. As we move through John's Gospel, we gradually come to learn how all of this came to be.

The Introduction of the Spirit (John 1)

In his very first chapter, John, our witness, dramatically introduces Jesus and the Spirit into his Gospel through the witness of John the Baptizer. The scene took place in Bethany across the Jordan where John was baptizing. As the Baptizer saw Jesus coming toward him, he declared: "Here is the Lamb of God who takes away the sin of the world! This is he of whom I said, 'After me comes a man who ranks ahead of me because he was before me.' I myself did not know him; but I came baptizing with water for this reason, that he might be revealed to Israel" (John 1:29–31). John continued testifying, "I saw the Spirit descending from heaven like a dove, and it remained on him. I myself did not know him, but the one who sent me to baptize with water said to me, 'he on whom you see the Spirit descend and remain is the one who baptizes with the Holy Spirit.' And I myself have seen and have testified that this is the Son of God" (John 1:32–34). From this early testimony in John's Gospel, we begin to grasp the concept that Jesus is the "Lamb of God who takes away the sin of the world" (John 1:29). And Jesus is the Son of God who is the one who baptizes with the Holy Spirit and "gives the Spirit without measure" (John 3:34).

The Spirit Is Key to God's Master Plan of Salvation (John 3)

John later introduces God's master plan of salvation to the world in his witness of the following discussion between Jesus and Nicodemus. One night in Jerusalem,

Nicodemus, a Pharisee and leader of the Jews, came to speak with Jesus. Nicodemus, who was aware of Jesus' signs, said to him, "Rabbi, we know that you are a teacher who has come from God; for no one can do these signs that you do apart from the presence of God" (John 3:2). Jesus responded, "Very truly, I tell you, no one can see the kingdom of God without being born from above" (John 3:3). And Nicodemus said, "How can anyone be born after having grown old? Can one enter a second time into the mother's womb and be born?" (John 3:4). And Jesus responded, "Very truly, I tell you, no one can enter the kingdom of God without being born of water and Spirit. What is born of the flesh is flesh, and what is born of the Spirit is spirit. Do not be astonished that I said to you, 'You must be born from above'" (John 3:5–7).

Nicodemus understood Jesus' signs for what they were — manifestations of the power and presence of God in the world — and recognized him as "a teacher who has come from God." Jesus responded by revealing to him that no one can see or enter the kingdom of God without receiving the Spirit from above. But Nicodemus misunderstood and thought that Jesus was talking about a rebirth of the flesh. Jesus then emphasized that flesh has its limits — "You must be born from above" — making it very clear that one must be born of the Spirit to enter into the kingdom of God.

Nicodemus remained puzzled with Jesus' response, but he persisted in attempting to better understand Jesus' revelation by asking him another question, which was his final question: "How can these things be?" Before answering his question, Jesus first discloses where he is from: "No one has ascended into heaven except the one who descended from heaven, the Son of Man" (John 3:13). Jesus, who calls himself the Son of Man, makes it clear that he has accessed both heaven and earth and has descended from heaven, thereby testifying to his unique relationship with God. Therefore, his knowledge "about heavenly things" (John 3:12) goes far beyond the knowledge of "a teacher who has come from God."

After establishing his authority, Jesus then answers the Pharisee's question about what must happen to allow one to be born of the Spirit from above. His answer is the following statement: "And just as Moses lifted up the serpent in the wilderness, so must the Son of Man be lifted up, that whoever believes in him may have eternal life" (John 3:14–15).

Jesus' answer to Nicodemus, "And just as Moses lifted up the serpent in the wilderness," is referring to a bronze serpent that was hoisted to the top of a long pole by Moses, as commanded by God, so as to save the lives of unfaithful Israelites from poisonous serpents (see Num. 21:4–9). If the Israelites looked up at the serpent seeking mercy from God, their lives would be saved. By comparing this event to his being lifted up in crucifixion, Jesus is implying that his crucifixion is a life-saving event. In the second part of his answer, "so must the Son of Man be lifted up," he is referring to his crucifixion, as well as to his resurrection and ascension. Being lifted up in crucifixion is the first of three dynamic sequential events whereby Jesus, the Son of Man, is also lifted up in resurrection and ascension to the Father (see chapter 10).[1] In the third and final part of his answer, "that whoever believes in him may have eternal life," Jesus is revealing to Nicodemus that those who believe in him will be born from above, will be born of the Spirit, and therefore will have life beyond the flesh and will see and enter the kingdom of God.

In the very next two verses following what Jesus had just revealed to Nicodemus, we find the summary of God's master plan of salvation: "For God so loved the world that he gave his only Son, so that everyone who believes in him may not perish but may have eternal life. Indeed, God did not send the Son into the world to condemn the world, but in order that the world might be saved through him" (John 3:16–17). And for this saving event to have occurred, Jesus had to follow through on God's plan, as indicated by the word *must*, as is found in "you must be born from above" and in "so must the Son of Man be lifted up." So Jesus not only revealed God's plan but also fulfilled it so that humanity may have the opportunity to be born of the Spirit and enter the kingdom of God.

Jesus' Glorification Must Occur for Humanity to Receive the Spirit (John 7)

It was the last day of the festival of Booths, and while at the temple in Jerusalem, Jesus cried out, "'Let anyone who is thirsty come to me, and let the one who believes in me drink. As the scripture has said, "Out of the believer's heart shall flow rivers of living water."' Now he said this about the Spirit, which believers in him were to receive; for as yet there was no Spirit, because Jesus was not yet glorified" (John 7:37–39). It is here that John further clarifies what must occur before humanity may receive the Spirit, the Spirit that is necessary to attain eternal life and is key to entering the kingdom of God. John makes it clear that for humanity to receive the Spirit, Jesus must be glorified: "For as yet there was no Spirit, because Jesus was not yet glorified." As stated in the Nicodemus narrative, in order to complete

God's plan of salvation for the human race, Jesus, the Son of Man, "must" be lifted up. Again, lifted up includes his crucifixion, resurrection, and ascension back to the Father. Here in John's Gospel the word *glorified* pertains to Jesus' "hour of glory" and encompasses the three separate events (crucifixion, resurrection, and ascension to the Father) into one major event.[2] At Jesus' glorification, the Spirit was then sent into our world of time and space, which allows those who believe to have life everlasting in Jesus' name.

The Hour of Glory Has Come (John 12)

It was just before the Passover when Jesus entered Jerusalem, which was crowded because of the upcoming festival. Many in the crowd had either seen or heard of Jesus' sign, "when he called Lazarus out of the tomb and raised him from the dead" (John 12:17). They had gathered to praise him as he entered the city. It was around that time that John our witness reports on what Jesus said about being glorified:

> The hour has come for the Son of Man to be glorified. Very truly, I tell you, unless a grain of wheat falls into the earth and dies, it remains just a single grain; but if it dies, it bears much fruit. Those who love their life lose it, and those who hate their life in this world will keep it for eternal life. Whoever serves me must follow me, and where I am, there will my servant be also. Whoever serves me, the Father will honor. (John 12:23–26)

Here Jesus voices that the time of his glorification has come and that it is his hour of glory that will bring eternal life to those who follow him.

The Son of Man Must Return to the Father (John 13)

John continues to reveal the story of God's plan of salvation during his narrative of the evening of the last supper. He begins by relating to his readers as to where Jesus is going after his death. "Now before the festival of the Passover, Jesus knew that his hour had come to depart from this world and go to the Father" (John 13:1). And it is after the last supper that Jesus reveals to his disciples more of God's plan that will bring salvation to the world through the Spirit: "But now I am going to him who sent me; yet none of you asks me, 'Where are you going?' But because I have said these things to you, sorrow has filled your hearts. Nevertheless, I tell you the truth: it is to your advantage that I go away, for if I do not go away, the Advocate [Spirit] will not come to you; but if I go, I will send him to you" (John 16: 5–7). Here again, it is key to understand that if Jesus did not follow God's plan, that the Son of Man "must" be lifted up in crucifixion, resurrection, and ascension to the Father, the Holy Spirit would not have been sent.

From Where the Spirit Comes (John 15)

From where does the Spirit come, the Spirit that can endow humanity with eternal life in the Kingdom of God? John gives more details of what he has heard from the Lord: "When the Advocate comes, whom I will send to you from the Father, the Spirit of truth who comes from the Father, he will testify on my behalf" (John 15:26). So indeed, the Spirit comes from God. It is God who gives humanity the Spirit, so that we may be born of the Spirit and become part of the eternal nature of God and become children of God in his kingdom for eternity. "But to all who received him, who believed in his name, he gave power to become children of God, who were born, not of blood or of the will of the flesh or of the will of man, but of God" (John 1:12–13).[3]

The Day Humanity Received the Holy Spirit (John 20)

John brings his narrative of the Spirit to its conclusion with two remarkable post-Resurrection events. The first event occurred early on the morning of the resurrection and ascension; Mary Magdalene had encountered the risen Jesus at the tomb. Jesus told her to tell his brothers that "I am ascending to my Father and your Father, to my God and your God" (John 20:17).[4, 5] Later in the evening of that same day, the second event occurred. The disciples of Jesus were hidden away in a house with locked doors for fear of being discovered by the Jewish religious authorities, who had just three days before crucified their Lord. Suddenly, the risen Jesus stood in their midst and greeted them, "Peace be with you" (John 20:19). His disciples rejoiced when they saw the Lord.

John's witness of the sequence of these two events tells his readers that the risen Jesus who now appeared in the locked room had recently returned from having ascended to his Father. During that same appearance in the locked room, Jesus again said to his disciples, "Peace be with you. As the Father has sent me, so I send you" (John 20:21). He then breathed on them and said, "Receive the Holy Spirit"

(John 20:22). So from then on, the Spirit that gives eternal life has been available to all who believe in the Son. God's plan, which had been presented by Jesus to Nicodemus, had now been completed by Jesus, the Son of God.

The Shroud — the Visual Confirmation of the Fulfillment of God's Plan of Salvation

The blood and image of the lifted man of the shroud points to God's plan of salvation. The blood marks alone tell us of the agony that the Lamb of God experienced to take away the sin of the world. The presence of the image of the lifted man tells us that God's plan of salvation exists in our world of time and space, and at the same time it confirms that God's plan was completed. Otherwise, there would be no upright image of the shroud. The Holy Spirit of eternal life, our gift from God, was paid for at the highest price imaginable. So, what does all this mean? It means that God's work, God's sign, that of the lifted Jesus of the shroud that we can see with our own eyes, *visually confirms* that Jesus' revelation of the Spirit, the Holy Spirit that gives humanity eternal life, is true. God is spirit (see John 4:24), there is a spiritual world, and there is everlasting life for all who follow him.

CHAPTER 14

Who God Is

GRADUALLY, BECAUSE OF what is visible on the shroud cloth, I began to realize more about who God is. Through Jesus' shroud and John's witness of Jesus' life, God is communicating personally to each one of us and is indeed telling us who he is. Yes, God is spirit, and he is the source of our gift of eternal life. But John has even more to say that brings us to a greater understanding of who God is: God is life, God is love, and God is true.

God Is Life

It was only because of my pursuit of the meaning of the upright man of the shroud that I finally came to realize that, just as John included the revelation of the Spirit throughout his entire Gospel, he also unfolded, from beginning to end, a parallel story of Jesus' works of creation, signs, that affirm that God is life. And most important, I came to realize how persistent our Creator is in wanting us to know who he is. We know this because John so carefully recorded the pertinent events. Right from the start of his Gospel, John tells us: "All things came into being through him, and without him not one thing came into being. What has come into being in him was life, and the life was the light of all people. The light shines in the darkness, and the darkness did not overcome it" (John 1:3–5). Here, John introduces Jesus as the Creator of all things and the source of life. Jesus is the light who brought into the world the light of life that was not overcome by darkness.

Jesus Is the Source of Life (John 5)

As John's witness unfolds, we find Jesus in a discussion with Jews of authority. Jesus said, "The works that the Father has given me to complete, the very works that I am doing, testify on my behalf that the Father has sent me. And the Father who sent me has himself testified on my behalf. You have never heard his voice or seen his form, and you do not have his word abiding in you, because you do not believe him whom he has sent" (John 5:36–38). And he went on to say,

> You search the scriptures because you think that in them you have eternal life; and it is they that testify on my behalf. Yet you refuse to come to me to have life. I do not accept glory from human beings. But I know that you do not have the love of God in you. I have come in my Father's name, and you do not accept me; if another comes in his own name, you will accept him. How can you believe when you accept glory from one another and do not seek the glory that comes from the one who alone is God? (John 5:39–44)

They were not seeking the glory that comes from the works of God the Father. As a result, they refused to come to Jesus to have life. They did not accept him.

Whoever Follows Jesus Will Have the Light of Life (John 8)

Another time while Jesus was teaching in the treasury of the temple, he said, "I am the light of the world. Whoever follows me will never walk in darkness but will have the light of life" (John 8:12). The Pharisees who were there argued with him, saying, "You are testifying on your own behalf; your testimony is not valid" (John 8:13). Jesus responded, "In your law it is written that the testimony of two witnesses is valid. I testify on my own behalf, and the Father who sent me testifies on my behalf" (John 8:17–18). Again, they did not accept him.

Jesus Is the Light of the World (John 9)

Yet another time, "As he walked along, he saw a man blind from birth" (John 9:1). He then said to his disciples, "'We must work the works of him who sent me while it is day; night is coming when no one can work. As long as I am in the world, I am the light of the world.' When he had said this, he spat on the ground and made mud with the saliva and spread the mud on the man's eyes, saying to him, 'Go, wash in the pool of Siloam....' Then he went and washed and came back able to see" (John 9:4–7). Through John's witness his readers come to understand the message of Jesus' work of God, in re-creating the eyes of this man who was blind from birth — Jesus is indeed "the light of the world," "the light of life." But again, the Pharisees did not accept him. [For more on the man blind from birth, see note 14.1.]

Jesus Is the Resurrection and the Life (John 11 and 12)

Still at another time, John witnessed to the raising of Lazarus. When Jesus met Martha, she said to him,

> "Lord, if you had been here, my brother would not have died. But even now I know that God will give you whatever you ask of him." Jesus said to her, "Your brother will rise again." Martha said to him, "I know that he will rise again in the resurrection on the last day." Jesus said to her, "I am the resurrection and the life. Those who believe in me, even though they die, will live, and everyone who lives and believes in me will never die." (John 11:21–26)

Again, it was a work of God — it was the manifestation of the presence and power of God that immediately re-created the body of Lazarus and brought him back to life.

This event gave John, and all the others who were there that day, the visual evidence, the sign, that Jesus was sent by the Father and that indeed Jesus is "the resurrection and the life." But John records yet again that the Jewish authority still did not accept him. "When the great crowd of the Jews learned that he was there, they came not only because of Jesus but also to see Lazarus, whom he had raised from the dead. So the chief priests planned to put Lazarus to death as well, since it was on account of him that many of the Jews were deserting and were believing in Jesus" (John 12:9–11).

The Hour Has Come for the Son of Man to Be Glorified (John 12 and 20)

So Jesus, the Son of God, persisted in following God's plan of salvation; he went on to pay the highest price so that we would all come to know who God is. Jesus said,

> The hour has come for the Son of Man to be glorified. Very truly,
> I tell you, unless a grain of wheat falls into the earth and dies, it

> remains just a single grain; but if it dies, it bears much fruit. Those
> who love their life lose it, and those who hate their life in this world
> will keep it for eternal life. Whoever serves me must follow me, and
> where I am, there will my servant be also. Whoever serves me, the
> Father will honor. (John 12:23–26)

This culminating event of his ministry — his death on the cross, followed by his
resurrection and ascension to his Father — was captured in a moment of time
when the image of his raised body was reflected onto his shroud.

And this visual evidence is available to us in our day. This image of the lifted
man of the shroud is a sign, a work by God revealing who Jesus is — the Son of the
Father. Indeed, this moment of glory — Jesus' resurrection and ascension — tells
the world that God is the light of life, God is life. This understanding comes to
all those who "seek the glory that comes from the one who alone is God" (John
5:44). "Now Jesus did many other signs in the presence of his disciples, which are
not written in this book. But these are written so that you may come to believe that
Jesus is the Messiah, the Son of God, and that through believing you may have life
in his name" (John 20:30–31).

God Is Love

The image of the upright man of the shroud visually communicates that God's
plan of salvation was accomplished through his Son. But what motivated God to
carry out a plan that would give humanity the Spirit, our source of eternal life?
John witnessed to what indeed motivated God: "For God so loved the world that
he gave his only Son, so that everyone who believes in him may not perish but
may have eternal life" (John 3:16). Yes, the motivation was love. And Jesus the
Son speaks of himself as fulfilling God's plan, God's work, because of his love for
the Father and for us. Jesus uses the imagery of the good shepherd who is willing
to die for his sheep:

> I am the good shepherd. I know my own and my own know me, just
> as the Father knows me and I know the Father. And I lay down my
> life for the sheep. I have other sheep that do not belong to this fold.
> I must bring them also, and they will listen to my voice. So there
> will be one flock, one shepherd. For this reason the Father loves
> me, because I lay down my life in order to take it up again. No one

takes it from me, but I lay it down of my own accord. I have power to lay it down, and I have power to take it up again. I have received this command from my Father. (John 10:14–18)

The relationship between the Father and the Son is one of love. "I do as the Father has commanded me, so that the world may know that I love the Father" (John 14:31). Love motivates the Father and the Son, who both give to humankind the Spirit of everlasting life "without measure" (John 3:34) (figure 14.1).

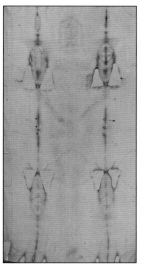 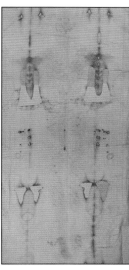

Figure 14.1:

"For this reason the Father loves me, because I lay down my life in order to take it up again. No one takes it from me, but I lay it down of my own accord. I have power to lay it down, and I have power to take it up again" (John 10:17–18).

"For this reason the Father loves me, because I lay down my life in order to take it up again" (John 10:17). Indeed, that is exactly what we see when we look at the blood marks and image of the lifted man of the shroud. Jesus laid down his life for humanity and took it up again to bring humanity to everlasting life through God's gift of the Spirit. And there is more.

John's witness of John the Baptizer brings out another dimension of Jesus' future suffering from the scourging and crucifixion inflicted by the human race. John, our witness, enlightened his readers of this dimension when he brought them to the scene in Bethany across from the Jordan where John was baptizing. As John the Baptizer saw Jesus coming toward him, he told those around him, "Here is the Lamb of God who takes away the sin of the world!" (John 1:29). Regarding sin, Jesus tells us, "Very truly, I tell you, everyone who commits sin is a slave to sin" (John 8:34). It is understood that sin is that which separates humanity from God. So just as the Baptizer said, the suffering of Jesus as the Lamb of God took away the sin of the world and brought humanity back to God. Jesus' act of humility, suffering, and death demonstrates the Son of God's profound love for the Father and for each person in the world. "Now before the festival of the Passover, Jesus knew that his hour had come to depart from this world and go to the Father. Having loved his own who were in the world, he loved them to the end" (John 13:1) (figure 14.2).

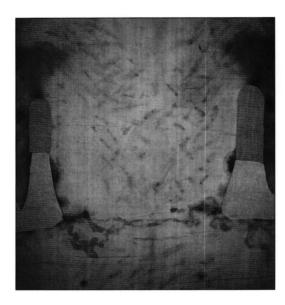

Figure 14.2: Scourge marks of the upper back widened by carrying a heavy load on the shoulders

"*Here is the Lamb of God who takes away the sin of the world!*" (*John 1:29*).

And later John tells us that Jesus said, "As the Father has loved me, so I have loved you; abide in my love. If you keep my commandments, you will abide in my love, just as I have kept my Father's commandments and abide in his love. I have said these things to you so that my joy may be in you, and that your joy may be complete" (John 15:9–11). Clearly, Jesus' words tell us that a relationship with God is a two-way commitment. But it is by taking up his cross for the sake of saving humanity that he tells us he loves each one of us no matter who we are or what we have done. Jesus communicates to us by his example, his words, and his works. The Son of God draws us to himself by his suffering, humility, and profound love. The blood marks and image on his shroud are a visual declaration of this suffering, humility, and profound love.

In John we find that Jesus has a very personal love for each of us. It was during the evening of the last supper, when Jesus told his disciples that he would be with them "only a little longer" (John 13:33). Toward the end Jesus reassured his disciples, saying, "Do not let your hearts be troubled. Believe in God, believe also in me. In my Father's house there are many dwelling places. If it were not so, would I have told you that I go to prepare a place for you? And if I go and prepare a place for you, I will come again and will take you to myself, so that where I am, there you may be also" (John 14:1–3). What John witnessed that night and passed on to his readers was the next step of God's plan. It is the remarkable story of what happens at the end of the life of the flesh for those who believe "in his name" (John 20:31). It is the next step that occurs at the very beginning of eternal life for those who are born of the Spirit. "I will come again and will take you to myself, so that where I am, there you may be also." It is here that we find that the Son of God personally prepares a place for us near him, and personally receives each believer into his Father's house. Yes, those deeds promised by Jesus reveal the personal love that God has for each of us. All of us will one day be facing death, and Jesus' assurance of life in the Father's house, the house of the humble and loving God, the creator of "all things" (John 1:3), has no equal. Yes, God is love.

God Is True

John was very capable of recording all the details of Jesus' crucifixion to the point that everything he witnessed is documented in great detail on the shroud. That was not an accident. Therefore, it would not be unusual for a man with such talent to have made the effort to document Jesus' last interrogations by Pilate just before the end. The conversation witnessed here elucidates further insights into who God is and why Jesus, the Son of God, came — he came to witness to the nature of God: God is true.

It was the day of the Crucifixion. The interrogation was just hours before Jesus died, was taken down from his cross, and was laid in his burial cloth. The event took place at Pilate's headquarters. He was deciding the fate of the Son of God. Pilate asked Jesus,

> "Are you the king of the Jews?" Jesus answered, "Do you ask this on your own, or did others tell you about me?" Pilate replied, "I am not a Jew, am I? Your own nation and the chief priests have handed you

over to me. What have you done?" Jesus answered, "My kingdom
is not from this world. If my kingdom were from this world, my
followers would be fighting to keep me from being handed over to
the Jews. But as it is, my kingdom is not from here." Pilate asked
him, "So you are a king?" Jesus answered, "You say that I am a king.
For this I was born, and for this I came into the world, to testify to
the truth. Everyone who belongs to the truth listens to my voice."
Pilate asked him, "What is truth?" (John 18:33–38)

Pilate then went out to the Jews, telling them, "I find no case against him" (John
18:38). But the interchanges and politics of the hour, which included Pilate's second
and final conversation with Jesus, still resulted in Jesus' crucifixion.

John brings us into the room to listen to a communication between two people.
Here, Jesus was not talking to another countryman, another Jew, but he was talking
to a Gentile that represented the world as it was. From the conversation, Pilate was
likely a man that had no interest in truth but only in survival politics so as to main-
tain power. That message was brought home in his words, "What is truth?" (John
18:38). But more important were the words of Jesus. Jesus held nothing back. Not
once but three times he told Pilate that his kingdom was not from this world. He
described his kingdom, his spiritual kingdom, to be outside of our world, as were
all of his works throughout his ministry. Therefore, it is no coincidence that all his
works, including the creation of the image of the lifted man of the shroud, were
also outside our ordinary understanding of space and time, outside of our world.

But most important is that in this conversation, Jesus witnesses to why he
was born and why he came from his spiritual kingdom into our world of space
and time. Jesus tells us that he came into the world "to testify to the truth." Here,
just before his death, Jesus is indicating the reason why he was sent by the Father.
Truth is of central importance to him, to the Father, to the Spirit, and to us. And
"everyone who belongs to the truth" listens to his voice. What is happening here?
Is it through truth that we connect to the living God? During his last supper, just
hours before his interrogation by Pilate, Jesus revealed that truth is part of his
nature: "I am the way, and the truth, and the life" (John 14:6). So by belonging
to the truth we connect to him and listen to his voice.

So now to answer Pilate's question: "What is truth?" Earlier on during Jesus'
ministry John tells us that Jesus was at the temple speaking with other Jews. The

conversation developed into an intra-Jewish debate that led to Jesus' answer concerning what truth is. He defined truth by differentiating it from its opposite — lies, deceit. Jesus said, "You are from your father the devil, and you choose to do your father's desires. He was a murderer from the beginning and does not stand in the truth, because there is no truth in him. When he lies, he speaks according to his own nature, for he is a liar and the father of lies" (John 8:44). The devil's nature holds no truth, so evil itself is the absence of truth.

Everyone who has had the unfortunate experience of being deceived knows the difference between truth and deception with truth being the reality[1] of how things are and deception being the lie, being evil. "For all who do evil hate the light and do not come to the light, so that their deeds may not be exposed. But those who do what is true come to the light, so that it may be clearly seen that their deeds have been done in God" (John 3:20–21). So according to John's witness of Jesus' life, deeds done in truth are done in God. Thus, by this insight, which Jesus has revealed and John has shared, we know how we may participate in God's light. By living a life doing what is true, we are doing our deeds in God. It is there that we can listen to his voice: "Everyone who belongs to the truth listens to my voice." And so, from John's witness, we come to understand that God is true.

CHAPTER 15

◇◇◇◇◇◇◇◇◇

The Hour of Glory

THE INVISIBLE GOD who is life, who is love, and who is true, has communicated to humanity through his Son, in words and works. John gradually brings us to the culminating event of Jesus' ministry, his "hour of glory," when Jesus is lifted up in crucifixion, resurrection, and ascension to his Father. This event was God's greatest work, a work that astonishes, a work that continues to visually communicate to the world today who Jesus is. How can that be? Because that "hour of glory" was reflected onto his Son's shroud, which is visually available to us today.

What has John, our witness, revealed to us about this "hour"? It was during the evening of the last supper and John was there as a witness to the words of Jesus. Jesus prepared the disciples for what was about to happen — his glorification. Jesus said in prayer to the Father: "I glorified you on earth by finishing the work that you gave me to do. So now, Father, glorify me in your own presence with the glory that I had in your presence before the world existed" (John 17:4–5). The goal of the hour of glory was for Jesus to return to his Father.[1] Once Jesus ascended to the Father in glory (see John 7:37–39 and 20:17), the Spirit of truth that gives us eternal life was sent to the world (see John 15:26, 16:5–7, and 20:22). It was all part of God's plan for the salvation of humanity. But there is much more about this hour that John shares with his readers.

John witnessed to what he himself experienced with Jesus. Jesus' revelations prepared John for the epiphany that he experienced when he entered the tomb that morning and saw the image of the raised body of his Lord. The first revelation was the sign that Jesus had predicted in the temple: "Destroy this temple, and in three days I will raise it up" (John 2:19). Yes, it was because of that prediction that John instantly believed that Jesus is the Son of God. But Jesus had also carefully prepared his disciples with more revelations that would better prepare them for what John would see as he entered the tomb. And now, as we read the Gospel of John, it becomes evident that, just as Jesus prepared his disciples for that moment, John had done the same: he prepared his readers for that moment in time when his readers would have the shroud in hand and would see what he saw: the image of the raised Jesus. John carefully prepared his Gospel so that in time everyone would experience what he experienced in the tomb: "he saw and believed" (John 20:8).

Other than the sign itself that Jesus stated in the temple, what else did Jesus say that prepared John so well for that moment when he entered the tomb? John witnessed to three other occasions when Jesus predicted that he would be lifted up. Each time that Jesus predicted he would be lifted up, he would reveal a message. Each message was different, giving his listeners a total of *three specific messages*. And I must admit that if it were not for the lifted man of the shroud, I would never have come to know anything about these messages. Moreover, it took me years to gradually understand what Jesus was saying. And what he was saying definitely implied that the fulfillment of these messages required not only his being lifted up in Crucifixion, but it also required his being lifted up in resurrection and ascension to his Father. Each and every time he spoke about being lifted up, he not only was predicting his hour of glory but was also telling the world the significance of what that event means for each and every one of us. His words confirmed who he is.

The first time Jesus spoke about being lifted up (already discussed in chapter 13) was during Jesus' meeting with Nicodemus when Jesus revealed the first message summarized here: "And just as Moses lifted up the serpent in the wilderness, so must the Son of Man be lifted up, that whoever believes in him may have eternal life" (John 3:14–15). So the *first message* is: whoever believes in him may have eternal life.

The second time Jesus spoke about being lifted up was when he was teaching in the temple, attempting to help the Jews understand who he is and that he was sent by the Father. As he did when speaking to Nicodemus, he was attempting to establish his close relationship to the Father by informing the Jews that he was from heaven: "You are from below, I am from above; you are of this world, I am not of this world" (John 8:23). But they did not understand him and asked, "Who are you?" (John 8:25). Jesus responded to their question, but "they did not understand that he was speaking to them about the Father. So Jesus said, 'When you have lifted up the Son of Man, then you will realize that I am he, and that I do nothing on my own, but I speak these things as the Father instructed me. And the one who sent me is with me; he has not left me alone, for I always do what is pleasing to him'" (John 8:27–29).

Speaking to the Jews on that day in the temple had been going nowhere. They did not understand who he was. So in the end, he spoke to them about a future event that he knew was to be his hour of glory. So what did he mean by the words "when you have lifted up the Son of Man"? This was his crucifixion. Following his crucifixion was his resurrection and ascension to the Father, all part of his hour of glory. Without the hour of glory, no one would have ever remembered the carpenter from Galilee. It was only the hour of glory that would bring the world to understand who he is — "then you will realize that I am he" — that he is the deity, that he is God![2] And he explains that he does nothing on his own ("I do nothing on my own"), that he does only what the Father tells him ("I speak these things as the Father instructed me"). And most important, the Father is always with him: "The one who sent me is with me; he has not left me alone." Why? Because he is the faithful Son: "I always do what is pleasing to him." So he tells the world that he is in the Father and the Father is in him (also see John 10:38 and 14:11). That is who he is. He is the presence of God in the world. He is God's Son. Indeed, his culminating sign, being raised up, tells the world who he is. And it is the reflection of that event, the sign, the work, that we can see today on his shroud. The lifted man of the shroud is the mirrored moment of that event. Therefore, the *second message* is: you will realize that I am he [God].

It was just before the Passover feast when John told us that Jesus spoke for the third time about his being lifted up. The crowd in Jerusalem was shouting "Hosanna" as Jesus entered on the back of a donkey. They were praising him because they had seen or heard of his work, that of raising Lazarus from the dead.

Some Greeks had come to the Passover festival and wished to speak to Jesus. His disciples Andrew and Philip went to Jesus to tell him of the visitors. Jesus responded, "The hour has come for the Son of Man to be glorified. Very truly, I tell you, unless a grain of wheat falls into the earth and dies, it remains just a single grain; but if it dies, it bears much fruit" (John 12:23–24). Here Jesus is telling of his hour of glory, which starts with the prediction of his death, but there is more beyond his death. He then goes on to say, "'Now my soul is troubled. And what should I say — "Father, save me from this hour"? No, it is for this reason that I have come to this hour. Father, glorify your name.' Then a voice came from heaven, 'I have glorified it, and I will glorify it again'" (John 12:27–28). Here Jesus is tempted to avoid his hour, which starts with the deliberate destruction of the visible, living temple of God — his body (see John 2:19). But in an instant he overcomes the temptation to not take up his cross and goes on to follow the commandment that his Father had given him.

The crowd had difficulty understanding what they heard from heaven, and Jesus responded to the people with the following answer: "This voice has come for your sake, not for mine. . . . And I, when I am lifted up from the earth, will draw all people to myself" (John 12:30, 32). Here again Jesus gives us his third message regarding his hour of glory: he will draw all people to himself. Obviously, no one would be drawn to a dead, crucified Galilean if there were no Resurrection and Ascension to the Father.[3] So it is the completion of his hour of glory that ultimately shows who Jesus is. This hour of glory will draw all people to Jesus (for further discussion, refer to the end of chapter 10). Thus, John witnesses to Jesus' *third message*: I will draw all people to myself.

In summary, God the Father, who glorified his Son (see John 8:54 and 17:1, 5), left the sign of the raised/lifted Jesus on his shroud that visually communicates these *three messages* to the world:

1.   Whoever believes in him may have eternal life.

2.   You will realize that I am he [God].

3.   I will draw all people to myself.

John saw and heard Jesus predict three times that he would be lifted up. Each prediction was associated with a message that was part of the fulfillment of his hour of glory. By the time John entered the tomb, Jesus had well prepared him for what he was about to see in the cave. It was the sign that Jesus predicted in the temple — the image of the body of his Lord, raised up in resurrection and ascension to the Father. This sign of the lifted man of the shroud is the reflection of his hour of glory.

◇◇◇◇◇◇◇◇◇◇

CHAPTER 16

The Bread of God

THE SHROUD IMAGE, the reflection of the hour of glory, plays an important role in John's narrative on the bread of life. Below are the events John witnessed that help us understand that Jesus offers the world the sign of his lifted image as a visual testimony that he is truly "the bread of God" (John 6:33).

John, our witness, tells us that the Passover festival was near. And it was by the Sea of Galilee that a large crowd, about five thousand, followed Jesus "because they saw the signs that he was doing for the sick" (John 6:2). And it was there, from five barley loaves and two fish, that Jesus passed out food for the many, and when all had finished eating, the remaining fragments filled twelve baskets. The people witnessed Jesus' sign and "were about to come and take him by force to make him king" (John 6:15). In response, Jesus withdrew to the mountain alone. The next day the crowd looked for him, and finally, after traveling by boat across the Sea of Galilee to Capernaum, they found him teaching in the synagogue (John 6:59).

As John witnessed,

> When they found him on the other side of the sea, they said to him,
> "Rabbi, when did you come here?" Jesus answered them, "Very truly,
> I tell you, you are looking for me, not because you saw signs, but
> because you ate your fill of the loaves. Do not work for the food that
> perishes, but for the food that endures for eternal life, which the Son
> of Man will give you. For it is on him that God the Father has set
> his seal." Then they said to him, "What must we do to perform the

works of God?" Jesus answered them, "This is the work of God, that you believe in him whom he has sent." So they said to him, "What sign are you going to give us then, so that we may see it and believe you? What work are you performing?" (John 6:25–30)

But before hearing Jesus' response, they gave him an example of a sign that they were aware of from heaven. They told Jesus of their ancestors who ate manna in the wilderness, "as it is written, 'he [Moses] gave them bread from heaven to eat'" (John 6:31). In response, Jesus said to them, "Very truly, I tell you, it was not Moses who gave you the bread from heaven, but it is my Father who gives you the true bread from heaven. For the bread of God is that which comes down from heaven and gives life to the world" (John 6:32–33).

John captured an important interchange between Jesus and the crowd who asked him for a sign so that they may see it and believe him. Their previous historic sign from God was manna, the "bread from heaven" that their ancestors ate in the wilderness. So what sign is Jesus now going to show them? This new sign from Jesus is food that does not perish but endures for eternal life. It is the food that the Son of Man will give them. And that food is "the true bread from heaven" that comes from the Father. "For the bread of God is that which comes down from heaven and gives life to the world" (John 6:33).

On first hearing of "the true bread from heaven," the crowd was receptive: "Sir, give us this bread always" (John 6:34). In response Jesus said, "I am the bread of life. Whoever comes to me will never be hungry, and whoever believes in me will never be thirsty" (John 6:35). And from then on, as the crowd heard more, their sentiments began to change. "Then the Jews began to complain about him because he said, 'I am the bread that came down from heaven.' They were saying, 'Is not this Jesus, the son of Joseph, whose father and mother we know? How can he now say, 'I have come down from heaven'?" (John 6:41–42). Later, "the Jews then disputed among themselves, saying, 'How can this man give us his flesh to eat?'" (John 6:52). Jesus responded, "Those who eat my flesh and drink my blood have eternal life, and I will raise them up on the last day; for my flesh is true food and my blood is true drink" (John 6:54–55). In final response to Jesus' teaching, many of his disciples said, "This teaching is difficult; who can accept it?" (John 6:60). In the end, "many of his disciples turned back and no longer went about with him" (John 6:66). But before they left him, Jesus who was "aware that his disciples were complaining about it, said to them, 'Does this offend you? Then what if you were to see the Son of Man ascending to where he was before? It is the spirit that gives life; the flesh is useless. The words that I have spoken to you are spirit and life'" (John 6:61–63).

John makes it clear that Jesus taught about the bread of life the very next day after he accomplished the major sign of feeding thousands with the fish and loaves. Yet one can sense, from the conversations and interchange, the bewilderment of those who heard for the first time, "Those who eat my flesh and drink my blood have eternal life." And Jesus also realized it was difficult, because he later asked the Twelve, "Do you also wish to go away?" (John 6:67). And Simon Peter answered, "Lord, to whom can we go? You have the words of eternal life. We have come to believe and know that you are the Holy One of God" (John 6:68–69).

John, our witness, paid much attention to the words of the disciples while they were talking among themselves. The disciples were saying: "This teaching is difficult; who can accept it?" (John 6:60). Jesus, being aware of their complaint, quickly addressed their dilemma with a question: "Does this offend you?" (John 6:61). Jesus then immediately followed his question with an alternative answer to their original question, the question that asked for a sign: "What sign are you going to give us then, so that we may see it and believe you?" (John 6:30). Instead of returning to his discussion of the sign of the bread of life — his body and blood — he gave them the following alternative sign: "Then what if you were to see the Son of Man ascending to where he was before? It is the spirit that gives life; the flesh is useless. The words that I have spoken to you are spirit and life" (John 6:62–63). Do these words of Jesus sound familiar? Yes, these words were also part of Jesus' conversation with Nicodemus (chapter 13). Jesus is offering his offended disciples an alternative sign, the one that he previously described to Nicodemus: What must happen for the Spirit of eternal life to be available to them? Jesus, the Son of Man, must be lifted up. And this is the very same sign that Jesus presented in the temple: "Destroy this temple, and in three days I will raise it up" (John 2:19).

The first time Jesus was explicitly asked for a sign, he was in the temple of Jerusalem. The second time he was in the synagogue of Capernaum. In the temple, the sign was that his destroyed body would be raised up, lifted up. In Capernaum, Jesus reveals more about the same sign: his destroyed body would be raised up, lifted up in ascension; rising, ascending to where he was before — to his Father and to our Father, to his God and to our God (John 13:1 and 20:17). On both occasions

Jesus, the Son of Man, describes his upward movement, all part of fulfilling the goal of his hour of glory. Both describe what we see on the shroud, a man who is lifted up above the earth, a man whose hair falls to his shoulders and whose feet do not touch the ground.

The image of the lifted man of the shroud, the visual reflection of his hour of glory, is exactly what Jesus described as the sign. This sign that he would be raised up was offered the first time to visually establish that he is the Son of the Father, the Son of God, and therefore has the right to cleanse the temple. This sign was then offered a second time to establish that he is "the bread of life" (John 6:35), the real body and blood of the Son of God.

Hopefully, all who are seeking the glory of God through Jesus' words and works, including the work that he has left us on his shroud, may come to realize that God is real, that the Spirit is real, that eternal life with God is real, and that "the bread of God" (John 6:33) is real. What joy! Otherwise, for humanity there would be no future. There would be nothing.

In summary, we, humanity, lifted Jesus up on a cross, and it is God who lifted him up in resurrection and ascension to himself. The blood of atonement and the image of the lifted man of the shroud are the reflection of his hour of glory — the crucifixion and death of Jesus and his resurrection and ascension to his Father. On this cloth we see the whole story of salvation.

Figure 16.1
"*Then what if you were to see the Son of Man ascending to where he was before?*" (*John 6:62*).

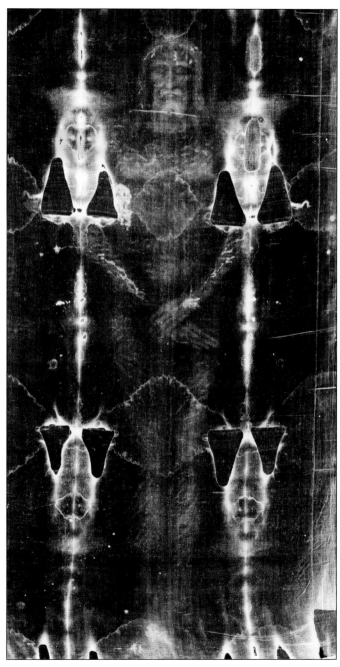

Figure 16.2

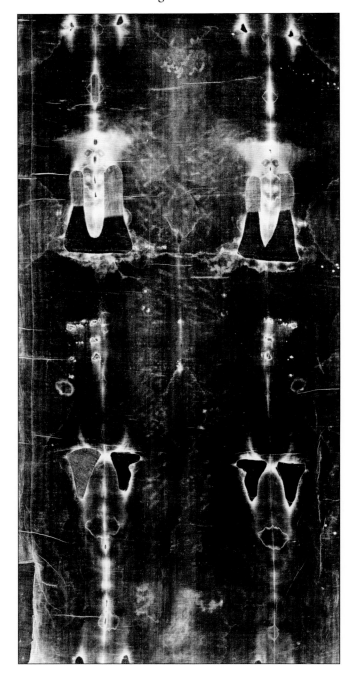

◇◇◇◇◇◇◇◇◇

Epilogue

"Believe me that I am in the Father and the Father is in me; but if you do not, then believe me because of the works themselves" (John 14:11).

IT WAS DURING that "hour of glory," in the darkness of the burial cave, that an event took place, the event that no one saw. "The light shines in the darkness, and the darkness did not overcome it" (John 1:5). Jesus' destroyed body was raised up. His body was glorified by his Father. "Father, the hour has come; glorify your Son so that the Son may glorify you," (John 17:1). The image of the raised man of the shroud is the reflection of this event. It is God's work, which visually communicates to the world that Jesus' predicted event took place: "Destroy this temple, and in three days I will raise it up" (John 2:19). And what data points us in this direction? The blood marks came first. The blood marks are absolutely consistent with those of a crucified dead man who has been taken down from his vertical position of crucifixion and placed supine on one end of this long cloth, and then covered by the other end. And within that cloth we see the blood marks that show that the man was buried in the supine position. Yet the image of the man is not in the supine position. His image is in the upright position with his hair falling to his shoulders and his feet not touching the ground. We see a destroyed man who has been raised up, a man who has been lifted up above the earth, lifted up in resurrection and ascension. This is the sign that Jesus, the Son of Man predicted each time he was asked for a sign, first at the temple in Jerusalem, and second, at the synagogue in Capernaum. This sign was offered the first time to visually establish that he is the Son of God, and the second time to establish that he is the bread of life.

God is at work, visually communicating to us through his Son's shroud and his Son's image — his Son's hour of glory: the crucifixion, resurrection, and ascension of his Son moving upward toward his Father. Yes, what you see is what you get. Set before us, in a captured moment in time, is the occurrence of the final dynamic event of the whole story of salvation, our salvation. "This is indeed the will of my Father, that all who see the Son and believe in him may have eternal life; and I will raise them up on the last day" (John 6:40). What we see on the shroud, the rising body of Jesus, "the Son of Man ascending to where he was before" (John 6:62), is exactly what will happen to all of us who believe in him. He who loved us "to the end" will raise us up "on the last day" and personally bring us into his Father's house where we shall live forever. "Do not let your hearts be troubled. Believe in God, believe also in me. In my Father's house there are many dwelling places. If it were not so, would I have told you that I go to prepare a place for you? And if I go and prepare a place for you, I will come again and will take you to myself, so that where I am, there you may be also" (John 14:1–3).

The Sign
(The Sculpture)

"Destroy this temple, and in three days I will raise it up" (John 2:19).

THE STUDY OF the two-dimensional image of the man of the Shroud of Turin resulted in the creation of the three-dimensional sculpture of the lifted man of the shroud as seen below. The visual confirmation that the man of the shroud is upright was the result of careful anatomical observations and study of the image. The cloth below his feet is simply an artistic concept of the shroud cloth falling from his body as he is rising.

The artist who created the sculpture is the internationally recognized sculptor Pablo Eduardo. I sought out Eduardo because he is a master of artistic anatomy. He took on this project because he agreed with the anatomical conclusion that the image of the man of the shroud is upright. On many occasions we worked together measuring, remeasuring, and using every single inch of the image and all the blood marks to best determine the three-dimensional anatomy of the shroud image. To achieve an optimal depth perspective, we made use of what look like the shadows of the image as a guide in reproducing similar shadows on the sculpture. These shadows are present in the ambient light of dawn or sunset. It was a productive, synergistic experience. We came to a better understanding of body-to-cloth contact and discovered several anatomical insights that resulted in a sculpture that comes very close to what is seen on the photographic negative of the original shroud image.

The major wounds of the image are part of the sculpture; however, there are no blood marks seen on the sculpture. The blood marks were not placed on the sculpture, because they were left behind on the shroud. We know this by the study of the blood marks and anatomy of the figure. One important example is the displacement of the blood marks from the face to the hair.

In contrast to the blood marks that show that the crucified man of the shroud was first laid out supine on his shroud, the anatomical form and the falling hair of the image show that his body is not supine. He is upright, lifted up as if in midair. The sculpture below is unique.

This sculpture of the man of the shroud visually shows that he is not lying in burial but is raised up, lifted up in resurrection and ascension to his Father. This sculpture of the Son of Man rising, ascending to his Father, is the sign that Jesus predicted at the temple in Jerusalem and at the synagogue in Capernaum. It is the sign that John saw in the tomb. This sculpture of the lifted man of the shroud gives us a three-dimensional view of God's message of salvation.

The Sign
"Destroy this temple, and in three days I will raise it up" (John 2:19).

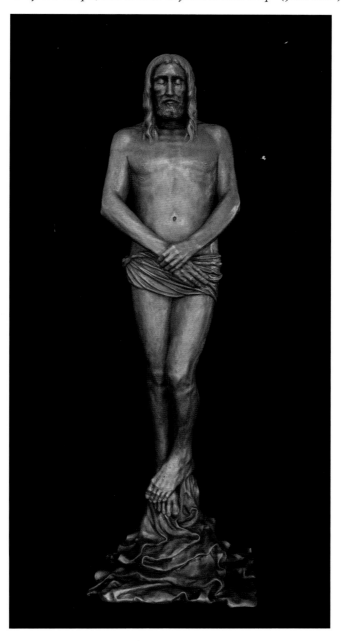

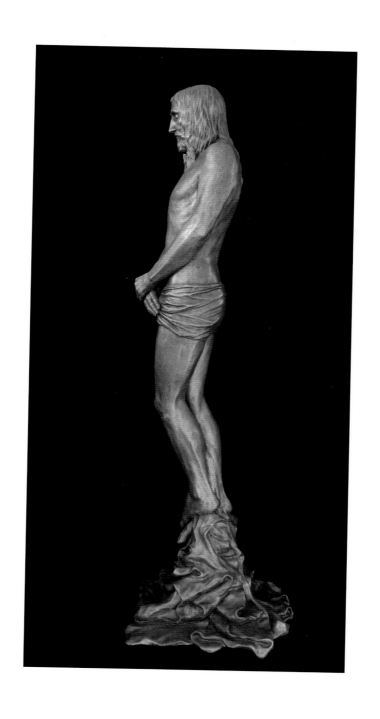

◇◇◇◇◇◇◇◇◇

Acknowledgments

WITHOUT THE HELP of many people this work would never have been accomplished. I must begin by thanking my wife, Bonnie Lavoie, for her patience over the years while I was preparing for this work. Moreover, as the manuscript was being written, Bonnie was there to read and constructively criticize each chapter. Indeed, she played a major role, and at the end stages she was again there for me, checking and rechecking every detail.

Then there was my first editor, Pam Travers, who took the manuscript to task and informed me as to what passages were simply not going to work for the reader. Plus, I also appreciated her insights on organizing the text. Evelyn Reilly, my second editor, did a beautiful job doing detailed editing. Most of all, I loved our robust discussions over some passages; they taught me so much. Her overall effort immensely improved the manuscript.

The final editor was my daughter Marguerite Cail. She is a professional editor who worked diligently to be sure that there was a logical sequence of ideas throughout the book. She also improved the wording. In the end, she made sure that the format of the manuscript was perfect for the publisher. She deserves a medal.

I must also add to this list others who participated in checking, adding to, and promoting the manuscript. I am very appreciative to Lynette Lewis, who helped with the introduction, and to my daughter Catherine Long, who gave her okay. I am grateful to Irene Sandler for her insight on a biblical verse and for her energy in promoting the project. Also, I appreciate Pat Fagan for his advice on a key transition paragraph. Moreover, I am very grateful for his suggestion and help in having

Scott Hahn and Mike Aquilina review my manuscript. I am most grateful to two of my former medical school colleagues, John Fisher and Leycester Owens, Jr., who worked with me reviewing medical insights regarding what likely led to the early death of the crucified Jesus. I most appreciate the efforts of my grandson William Cail, who patiently worked on a project in preparation for taking two photographs for the book. I wish to thank Mike Verbois for passing on his photographic insights on how we visualize people in our daily lives and for sharing with me a short history on Vernon Miller's career. Bob Joyce did a careful review of the manuscript that resulted in several corrections and offered insights for which I am most appreciative. Also, I am very grateful to Gene Zurlo, who took the time to study the manuscript, and most important, I appreciate the practical advice that he gave me during this entire project as well as helping me share my manuscript with Fr. Francis Hoffman. And I also appreciate the help of his daughter, Luanne Zurlo, who introduced me to her publisher, Sophia Institute Press, who published this work.

Of course, I sent the book out to those who had a good deal of knowledge of the Gospel of John. Even though I had taken two years of graduate work in biblical studies and then spent well over ten years carefully studying the Gospel of John, I knew it was important to have those with professional proficiency check my work. The first was Fr. George Szal, whom I've known for many years. He thought that the scriptural logic was correct but advised me to move on to others who had more scholarship than he. I very much appreciated his time and his advice.

I then brought the manuscript to Fr. Jurgen Liias, a true scholar of the Gospels. I had heard him give lectures on a number of occasions. I knew him but he did not know me. However, he was most gracious and read my manuscript. He made suggestions and was responsible for having me add a new section to one of the chapters. I am so appreciative for his time in being certain that my work was on track from a scriptural perspective. He also wrote a wonderful commentary that I very much appreciate and continue to use. I am also very grateful for his help in the process of getting my manuscript published.

Fr. Edward Healey, who has great knowledge of the Gospel of John, also willingly read my manuscript. He, as did the others, also understood the logic of the work and assured me that all the dots were connected correctly from a scriptural perspective. He also helped bring the manuscript in line with the present-day discernment of the scriptural world. For all this, I am most grateful.

Several of my colleagues who studied the shroud for many years have been most cooperative in helping me with the manuscript in different ways; thank you! Joe Marino gave me his time and helped me with some literature searches. Also, he was generous in allowing me to incorporate links to some of his shroud bibliographies into the book. Giulio Fanti graciously permitted me to use one of his photos. I am most grateful to Robert Rucker who pitched in and wrote a short summary for the book on the current hypotheses of image formation. Russ Breault kindly advised me to check the public domain for a photo that I needed. Ian Wilson graciously gave me advice regarding some historic data that I was considering using in the manuscript. I am also grateful to Tom McAvoy for his expertise and time in writing a short review for the book on the new technology (X-ray method) for dating ancient linen. I also appreciate how quickly Paolo Di Lazzaro responded in following up on a request that I had regarding permission to use an article on his site. And of course, I am most appreciative to Tom and Donna D'Muhala for their ongoing cooperation in the use of the photographs from the Vernon Miller collection.

I must also mention that during these past forty years as a student of the Shroud of Turin, I have had the great pleasure of meeting and knowing many of the individuals whose work I have discussed in this book. I thank them all for their insights and contributions in bringing to the world a better understanding of the Shroud of Turin.

Regarding the work of the sculpture mentioned in this book, I want to thank Pablo Eduardo, the sculptor who graciously allowed me to join him in his studio on numerous occasions, for hours at a time, over a three-year period, for the purpose of replicating the man of the shroud. Of course, full credit goes to Pablo Eduardo for creating a magnificent work, bringing the man of the shroud into our three-dimensional world. I also want to thank his staff and Camille Vicenti, who intermittently brought to us new insights as the work progressed. She is also responsible for the beautiful photos of the sculpture that are in this book. I also want to mention Digby Veevers-Carter, the man who did wonderful work casting the sculpture into bronze. And very important, I wish to thank my friend, Geoffrey FitzGerald who recently passed on to the Lord, and also thank his lovely wife, Janice for introducing me to Pablo Eduardo. Additionally, I want to thank Monica Toraldo, Joumana Cafferty, George Olson, Larry Cirignano, John Spadaccini, and Fr. John Arens for their help as well. And of course I want to thank my wife and children for all their support and input during the journey to the completion of the sculpture and the publication of the book.

It is now my pleasure to thank Charlie McKinney, the president of Sophia Institute Press, for taking on my work. I also want to thank Michael Warren Davis for his time in reading my manuscript, as well as Jean-Pierre Tetreault who gently guided me along in the process of becoming an author at Sophia. It has been a pleasure working with Anna Maria Dube who has been immensely helpful in answering all my questions regarding the final editing of the manuscript and the production of the book. And I must thank Rachael Clements for all her help in doing the final edits of the manuscript as well as Heather Houle for all her help. Overall, working with all the staff has been an enjoyable, productive experience.

Without the prayerful support of my father, Aurel G. Lavoie, M.D., my mother, Marguerite C. Lavoie, and Fr. Walter M. Abbott, S.J., this work would have never been accomplished.

Notes and References

Chapter 1: Introduction

1. L. De Caro et al., "X-ray Dating of a Turin Shroud's Linen Sample," *Heritage* 5, no. 2 (April 2022): 860–870.

Note 1.1: More on History

It was 1979 when I called Harvard University and asked for the name of a professor who was a specialist in iconography, the study of religious images. I was given the name of Dr. Ernst Kitzinger, who had spent a lifetime studying ancient paintings of Jesus from both the East and the West. I was fortunate to meet with him just before his permanent departure to England, where he planned to retire.

I asked Dr. Kitzinger the following question: "Can you show me some works of artists who have painted blood marks like the ones that you see on the Shroud of Turin?" His response was: "The Shroud of Turin is unique in art. It doesn't fall into any artistic category. For us, a very small group of experts around the world, we believe that the Shroud of Turin is really the Shroud of Constantinople. You know that the crusaders took many treasures back to Europe during the thirteenth century, and we believe that the shroud was one of them. As for the blood marks done by artists, there are no paintings that have blood marks like those of the shroud. You are free to look as you please, but you won't find any." I did look, and he was right; I have never found any. Nor has anyone else.

Over the years, many history scholars have been working to connect as many dots as possible as to where the shroud was prior to the 1350s. I had the pleasure of meeting Ian Wilson, one of the leading shroud historians, in Turin in 1978. He is still uncovering more new data and is now preparing a new book. For a list of Wilson's articles and books and for more historic information by many fine shroud historians, a link to an extensive list of English-language references is provided below. This list was compiled and is kept current by Joe Marino, who is a professional Shroud of Turin bibliographer.

REFERENCES FOR NOTE 1.1

> Joe Marino, "Possible Post-Biblical and Pre-1350s References in History to the Shroud of Jesus: An English-Language Bibliography," https://www.academia.edu/45402479/Possible_Post_Biblical_ and_Pre_1350s_References_in_History_to_the_Shroud_of_Jesus_an_English_language_Bibliography.

Note 1.2: More on Dr. Max Frei and His Pollen Study

While in Turin in 1978, I met Dr. Max Frei, a professor of criminology from the University of Zurich. He was a biologist whose specialty was using microscopic techniques in the field of criminology. He had discovered pollen grains on the shroud and thus was able to give it a geographical history (pollen grains are fine powdery microspores that take to the air in order to fertilize their own species). It had been years since I had thought about pollen, and my most recent encounter with it was in the form of a fine yellow-green film that covered my car during the warm season of the year. Following his talk, I approached him and took the opportunity to ask him about his presentation. In fluent English he responded: "It took me five years of my own time to do this work." As he spoke, he pointed to his chest with swift, rapid motions. He spoke with a satisfied smile, and I could sense the enthusiasm that he felt for his work.

In 1982, I read his paper. Here are some excerpts from his study:

> In 1973, together with two other experts, I was invited by the Archbishop of Turin to compare the structure of the Shroud's tissue, as seen on the photographs taken in 1969, with the original structure of the weave itself. I then discovered under my microscope a certain amount of dust between the linen threads.
>
> I requested and was given the permission to take samples of this dust by means of adhesive tape. . . .

It was a very difficult task to identify the different pollen-grains in the dust collected. First, I had to extract them from the sticking-tape and after cleansing they were embedded in glycerin jelly as permanent mountings, so that they could be studied from all sides under the light-microscope. The only true scientific method for identification of pollen-grains is the direct comparison with a mounting in the same medium of ripe pollen collected from a species to which the unknown pollen might belong.

The main problem in this procedure is to find out the right varieties for comparison. Fruitful ideas for comparison often originate from the study of books and articles with clear pollen pictures. A good help is the microscopical examination of all pollens available from private collections or public herbariums. In the case of the Shroud, all these sources gave only very few positive results. So I was obliged to make systematic studies of pollen-producing plants growing in such countries where the Shroud — supposing it was authentic — might have been contaminated. A positive identification of such pollens would be a confirmation of the Shroud's stay in that particular botanical region, while negative results concerning the whole flora of a country would allow the exclusion of the geographical area in question as source of contamination.[1]

Frei's words, "confirmation of the Shroud's stay in that particular botanical region," caused me to think of the shroud as a cloth that carried its own passport. Instead of the stamp of the custom's official naming the country of entrance, there were the pollens that clung to the cloth allowing Frei to determine its itinerary. Frei's own words best tell us what he discovered:

From 1974 to 1978, I traveled several times (in different floral seasons) through Palestine, Turkey (especially Anatolia and the region around Constantinople), through Cyprus, France and Italy, collecting pollens for direct comparison under the microscope. I devoted all my spare time to these journeys and the consequent laboratory work....

I succeeded in identifying 57 different plants which have left microscopical evidence on the Shroud.... Every identification has

been controlled not only under the optical microscope at magni-
fications ranging from 60x to 1200x, but also under the scanning
electron microscope....

> None of the pollens was glued to the cloth with tempera or
> covered with tempera. This is strong evidence against the possibility
> of the Shroud's being a painted fake.[2]

Frei found desert plants that grow in soils that have a high concentration of salt.
Many of these plants grow around the Dead Sea and are not found in Italy and
France. He found plants of rocky hills that grow in Israel and neighboring countries
(two still grow on the walls of ancient Jerusalem). He found Mediterranean plants
that grow in Israel as well as in France and Italy. He found plants from Anatolia
as well as some from Constantinople (Istanbul). He found plants that are widely
distributed in central Europe (France and Italy). He found no plants from Cyprus.[3]
Frei concluded that

> plants on the Shroud from Palestine and Anatolia are so numerous,
> compared to the species from Europe, that a casual contamination
> or a pollen-transport from the Near East by storms in different sea-
> sons cannot be responsible for their presence, as I have explained in
> several conferences and publications. The predominance of these
> pollens must be the result of the Shroud's stay in such countries
> where these plants form part of the normal vegetation.[4]

Frei leaves us with two very interesting pieces of information: (1) Even though
the known history of the shroud is confined to France and Italy from the 1350s
on, with Frei's pollen study we now know that the shroud did have an earlier Asian
and Palestinian history that preceded the 1350s. This history was either unknown
or for some reason never passed on by its first recorded European owner, Geoffrey de Charny. (2) Frei found no tempera on the pollens of the shroud. This was
significant in that he took some of his sticking-tape samples directly from the
shroud image in 1973. Frei felt that this was strong evidence against the shroud
image being a painting.

Frei's itinerary of the shroud, as determined by the pollens, also coincides with
Ian Wilson's theories as to the whereabouts of the shroud prior to the 1350s. [For
more on Ian Wilson, see note 1.1.]

The reliability of Frei's work has been recently confirmed by others.[5] See figure 1.4: photo of pollen grain and further discussion on the pollen grain shown.[6]

REFERENCES FOR NOTE 1.2

1. Max Frei, "Nine Years of Palynological Studies on the Shroud," *Shroud Spectrum International no.* 3 (June 1982): 3, https://www.shroud.com/spectrum.htm.

2. Ibid., 5.

3. Ibid., 5–7.

4. Ibid., 7.

5. G. Fanti and P. Malfi, *The Shroud of Turin* (Singapore: Jenny Stanford Publishing, 2015), 287–290.

6. Ibid., 289–290.

Note 1.3: More on Textile Evidence

Mechthild Flury-Lemberg, a well-known ancient textile expert, completed the Shroud of Turin restoration in 2002. I had the pleasure of meeting with her at her home in Bern, Switzerland, in 2010. Per her observations, this cloth was professionally produced on a large loom. And most important, the production method of this cloth is totally compatible with those made in the Middle East during the first century AD.

She concluded that the long, thin strip of cloth, which runs along most of one side of the shroud cloth, had to have been done when the shroud was made, in that this narrow strip of cloth is identical in all respects to the larger shroud cloth. The two separate pieces were sewn together by hand by a professional. She noted that the stitches of this unique seam were hardly visible from the front of the cloth. Of major importance, she mentioned the discovery of comparable stitches found in ancient Masada. In her article referenced below she wrote: "Also for this special design of the longitudinal seam, comparisons can be found on fabric fragments from the mentioned discovery from Masada."[1] With this discovery, the stitches of this seam became archeologically important.

Byzantine coins and the Sudarium of Oviedo are two other examples of several archeological/historical items used as evidence to document the pre-AD 1350 existence of the shroud. Two recent references on these subjects are included below.[2, 3.]

REFERENCES FOR NOTE 1.3

1. Mechthild Flury-Lemberg, "The Turin Shroud: Past, Present, Future; International Scientific Symposium, Torino, 2–5 March 2000," in *Sindon*, 24–25, 34–35.

2. Fanti, Giulio, *Byzantine Coins Influenced by the Shroud of Christ*, Jenny Stanford Series on Christian Relics and Phenomena, Vol. 3 (Singapore: Jenny Stanford Publishing Pte. Ltd., 2022).

3. Barta, Cesar, *The Sudarium of Oviedo, Signs of Jesus Christ's Death*, Jenny Stanford Series on Christian Relics and Phenomena, Vol. 4 (Singapore: Jenny Stanford Publishing Pte. Ltd., 2022).

Note 1.4: More on Carbon Dating

The public's confidence in the 1988 carbon dating results, which placed the origin of the Shroud of Turin cloth to sometime between 1260 and 1390, has been diminishing in the last several years for good reasons. First, the 1988 carbon dating study dates the origin of the shroud cloth to the Middle Ages. This study virtually stands alone against abundant data that points to a first-century event. Some of that data is documented in this book. Second, other dating tests mentioned in this chapter confirm that the time period of the life of Jesus falls within the time span of the cloth's origin.

Many of the books and scientific articles for and against the shroud being a fourteenth-century entity are available and periodically updated in the link below. The link is available through the effort of Joe Marino, a professional Shroud of Turin bibliographer. Joe has also documented the details of the history of the 1988 carbon-14 dating tests in his recent book, also referenced in this bibliography.[1]

Finally, the following article from the bibliography is suggested because it concentrates directly on recently available raw data from the 1988 carbon dating test: Tristan Casabianca et al., "Radiocarbon Dating of the Turin Shroud:

New Evidence from Raw Data," *Archaeometry* 61 (2019), no. 5: 1223–1231. In the abstract it states: "A statistical analysis of the *Nature* article and the raw data strongly suggests that homogeneity is lacking in the data and that the procedure should be reconsidered." The study concludes: "The statistical analyses, supported by the foreign material found by the laboratories, show the necessity of a new radiocarbon dating to compute a new reliable interval. This new test requires, in an interdisciplinary research, a robust protocol. Without this re-analysis, it is not possible to affirm that the 1988 radiocarbon dating offers 'conclusive evidence' that the calendar age range is accurate and representative of the whole cloth."[2]

REFERENCES FOR NOTE 1.4

1. Joe Marino, "The Radiocarbon Dating of the Turin Shroud in 1988 and Its Aftermath: An English-Language Bibliography," https://www.academia.edu/48831028/The_Radiocarbon_ Dating_of_the_Turin_Shroud_in_1988_and_its_After- math_an_English_language_Bibliography.

2. Tristan Casabianca et al, "Radiocarbon Dating of the Turin Shroud: New Evidence from Raw Data," *Archaeometry* 61 (2019), no. 5: 1223–1231.

Note 1.5: *More on the First Three Dating Methods*

In their book *The Shroud of Turin,* the authors Fanti and Malfi report the develop-ment of three new testing techniques for dating linen fibers that have been used to date the shroud. These three new techniques are totally distinct from the car-bon-14 test originally used to date this cloth. Chapters 6 and 7 of their book give the details of the development and basic information of each testing technique as well as the reliability of each test.

In summary, there are three tests. Two are chemical methods: the first chemical method is based on Fourier transform infrared (FT-IR), and the other chemical method is based on Raman vibrational spectroscopy. The third is a mechanical dating method for flax fabrics identified as a mechanical multiparametric dating method (MMPDM). Each of these three dating techniques depends on the certain specific changes in flax fibers that occur over time. Because these changes are time related, it is possible to derive their dates of origin. The dates of origin of the flax fibers from the shroud for each test are as follows: FT-IR age = 300 BC plus or minus 400 years, Raman age = 200 BC plus or minus 500 years, MMPDM age = AD 400 plus or minus 400 years. The final date of the shroud cloth, from analysis of the different methods combined, corresponds to 33 BC plus or minus 250 years at a confidence level of 95 percent. The authors note that the FT-IR dating has been corrected for the bias due to the shroud's exposure to fire in Chambery, France, in 1532.[1]

When challenged on the traceability of his shroud samples used for testing the date of the shroud, Fanti confirmed the authenticity of his samples in an article published in the *National Catholic Register*.[2]

REFERENCES FOR NOTE 1.5

1. G. Fanti and P. Malfi, *The Shroud of Turin* (Singapore: Jenny Stanford Publishing, 2015), 185–246, 284–286.

2. S. Parker, "Science Shines New Light on Shroud of Turin's Age," *National Catholic Register*, May 6, 2013, https://www.ncregister. com/news/science-shines-new-light-on-shroud-of-turin-s-age.

Note 1.6: More on the Fourth and Most Recent Test

The fourth test, the most recent one, is an X-ray dating method developed by Liberato De Caro, a scientist from Italy's Institute of Crystallography of the National Research Council in Bari. De Caro and his colleagues first presented their dating method in 2019.[1] He then applied his new dating technique to the shroud. In 2022[2] De Caro reported that the shroud linen is two thousand years old. I asked Tom McAvoy, Ph.D. in chemical engineering, who has expertise in this area of science, to comment on De Caro's articles. His comments are as follows:

"In a recent article,[1] De Caro et al. proposed a new method for dating ancient linen threads by inspecting their structural degradation using wide-angle X-ray scattering. Important characteristics of this new method are that it is non-destructive and that it can be applied to sub-millimeter-sized samples. Thus, multiple measurements can be made on a sample and their results averaged to give a more accurate estimate of its age compared to the case where only a single measurement is made.

Since the new dating method is non-destructive, a sample is unaltered and it can be tested by other dating methods, e.g., radiocarbon dating. De Caro et al. developed their method on nine linen samples ranging in age from 3000–3500 BC to the present time. The authors derived an equation for dating linen samples directly from wide-angle X-ray scattering measurements. Comparisons are given that show that the new dating method agrees very well with radiocarbon dating results. The new dating method requires that some environmental conditions need to hold and it can only be used on samples not older than 1000 BC.

"In a follow-up paper[2] De Caro applied the new X-ray scattering method to a small sample of linen taken from the Shroud of Turin. The size of the sample tested was approximately .5 mm by 1 mm. A total of eight measurements were made on the Shroud sample and their results were averaged. Depending on the environmental conditions to which the Shroud was exposed, its age was estimated from wide angle X-ray scattering to be between 19.3 and 21 centuries old. This age range agrees with the ages discussed in note 1.5 for the Shroud. An interesting conclusion from the paper[2] is that if the Shroud had not been brought to Europe during medieval times but it had been stored in a warmer climate, e.g., Turkey or Israel, its image may have disappeared by the present time due to degradation effects resulting from the higher temperatures. The colder temperature in Europe may have contributed to the Shroud's image still being visible today."

(Tom McAvoy is currently professor emeritus at the University of Maryland. He holds joint appointments in the Department of Chemical and Biomolecular Engineering, the Institute for Systems Research, and the Bioengineering Department. He has published more than 190 technical papers.)

In conclusion, the four shroud dating test results presented in notes 1.5 and 1.6 confirm that the time period of the life of Jesus falls within the time span of the cloth's origin.

REFERENCES FOR NOTE 1.6

1. L. De Caro et al., "X-ray Dating of Ancient Linen Fabrics," *Heritage* 2, no. 4 (November 2019): 2763–2783.

2. L. De Caro et al., "X-ray Dating of a Turin Shroud's Linen Sample," *Heritage* 5, no. 2 (April 2022): 860–870.

Chapter 2: Discovery: The Hidden Image

1. Ian Wilson, *The Shroud of Turin* (New York: Doubleday, 1978), 13–14.

2. Pierre Barbet, *A Doctor at Calvary* (New York: Doubleday, 1953), p. 8. The burn marks were the result of a fire that took place in 1532 at the Holy Chapel of Chambery, France, where the cloth was kept. The fire caused some of the silver chest to melt and molten metal burned through the folded cloth that lay within. The melted silver caused the parallel burn marks that enclose the body image of the cloth. Water was used to douse the flames, saving the cloth, but leaving water [calcium] rings all along the image area of the cloth. [Later, the holes were patched, and a backing cloth was added to stabilize the shroud. These patches were removed, and the old backing cloth was replaced during the restoration of 2002.]

3. "Quick Tour," https://shroudphotos.com/.

Chapter 3: The Gospel of John and the Blood Marks on the Shroud

1. Pierre Barbet, *A Doctor at Calvary* (New York: Doubleday, 1953).

2. Ibid., 92.

3. Ibid.

4. Ibid., 91. Multiple facial wounds described by Barbet.

5. Ibid., 107.

6. Ibid., 103 and 124. There are some early examples of art forms showing the nail through the wrist. The most famous is the Gero Crucifix of Cologne from the tenth century (personal communication with Dorothy Crispino, editor of *Shroud Spectrum International*).

7. Ibid., 110–112.

8. Ibid., 118.

9. Ibid., 119.

10. Ibid., 211.

11. Ibid., 97–98. Barbet speaks of the changes of the scourge marks being at the right shoulder area, but with UV enhancement one can see that the changes are at both shoulders (upper back, right and left).

12. Vernon Miller and S. F. Pellicori, "Ultraviolet Fluorescence Photography of the Shroud of Turin," *Journal of Biological Photography* 49, no. 3 (July 1981): 82.

Note 3.1: More on "Blood and Water"

Robert Bucklin, M.D., was a pathologist who studied the shroud for many years. He and I had the opportunity to discuss the pathophysiology of the death of the man of the shroud from the perspective of what we independently observed on the shroud as well as from John's witness, that blood and water came from Jesus' side following the lance wound. From my medical experience and from his experience as a pathologist, we had separately come to the same conclusion: the man of the shroud died in congestive heart failure.

Below are some quotes of Dr. Bucklin's thoughts that come from his article on the crucifixion of the man of the shroud.

> An accumulation of fluid in the pleural space without hemorrhage is a logical conclusion as a result of congestive heart failure related to the position of the victim on the cross. It is quite possible that there was a considerable amount of fluid so accumulated, enough so that when the lance pierced the side that fluid would be clearly seen.... If the theory of pleural effusion plus puncture of the right side of the heart were sustained, it would be expected that the water would have been visible from the side before the blood.[1]
>
> When the body was removed from the cross and placed in a horizontal position, there was a second large outflow of blood from the wound in the side. Much of this must have fallen onto the ground but some stayed on the body and flowed around the right side, leaving a large imprint of clot and serum in the lumbar area. It is in this imprint where the mixture of the blood and the watery fluid is best seen and its presence on the back lends further support to the theory that there was a pleural effusion rather than the water having come from the pericardial sack.[1]

Dr. Bucklin determined that the watery fluid was not pericardial fluid as some other physicians had concluded. Rather it was pleural fluid secondary to congestive heart failure. In his words, "However, the amount of pericardial fluid normally present is in the nature of 20 to 30 cubic centimeters, too small an amount to be seen by the naked eye as it came out of the wound in the side with the blood from the heart."[1]

Without the blood loss from the head wounds and the fluid and blood loss from the full body scourging, death by crucifixion alone would have taken much longer, and the final stages leading to death would have likely been different.

Dr. Bucklin stated, "A victim supported only by his wrists was unable to survive for more than a very short period of time; by having some kind of foot support, he was able to alternate his position so that his agony could be prolonged for a much greater period of time."[1]

The following study from another article gives more details: "Experiments conducted by Mödder (1948), in which healthy medical students were hung by the wrists, revealed signs of decompensation within 12 min. as the blood pressure halved, tidal volume decreased by 70%, and pulse pressure doubled. Breathing at this stage, with arms fully extended, was purely diaphragmatic. When the subjects were allowed to use their legs to lift the torso against gravity, the cardiovascular symptoms improved until the muscles fatigued and the vicious cycle continued."[2] This study also helps one to medically understand why breaking the legs of the crucified leads to a much quicker death.

If the feet are supported, then the agony continues for a longer period, a day or longer. Finally, the muscles of the legs fatigue; one can no longer push upward to enhance breathing, and death ensues by the inability to breath normally (exhaustion asphyxia).

REFERENCES FOR NOTE 3.1

1. Robert Bucklin, "The Medical Aspects of the Crucifixion of Our Lord Jesus Christ: From a Study of the Shroud of Turin," *The Linacre Quarterly* 25, no. 1 (February 1958): 5–14, https://epublications.marquette.edu/lnq/vol25/iss1/13.

2. Stephen Bordes et al., "The Clinical Anatomy of Crucifixion," *Clinical Anatomy* 33, no. 1 (2020): 12–21.

Chapter 4: Forbidden Images

1. Pierre Barbet, *A Doctor at Calvary* (New York: Doubleday, 1953), 6–7.

2. Flavius Josephus, *The Life and Works of Flavius Josephus*, trans. by William Whiston (Philadelphia: David McKay, n.d.) "Wars of the Jews," book 2, chapter X, 1, 3, and 4, 678–679.

3. *The Mishnah,* trans. by Herbert Danby (Oxford: Oxford University Press, 1933), Fourth Division, Nezikin, Tractate: Abodah Zarah 3[1], 440.

Chapter 5: The Shroud under a Microscope

1. John Jackson, Eric Jumper, and William Ercoline, "Correlation of Image Intensity on the Turin Shroud with the 3-D Structure of a Human Body Shape," *Applied Optics* 23, no. 14 (July 15, 1984): 2247.

2. Ibid., 2249.

3. Outstanding American scientific journal articles from shroud investigations done in 1978 are below. They are very technical and collectively demonstrate that the shroud is not a painting:

   a. L. A. Schwalbe and R. N. Rogers, "Physics and Chemistry of the Shroud of Turin: A Summary of the 1978 Investigation," *Analytica Chimica Acta* 135, no. 1 (February 1982): 3–49.

   b. J. H. Heller and A. D. Adler, "A Chemical Investigation of the Shroud of Turin," *Canadian Society of Forensic Science Journal* 14, no. 3 (1981): 81–103.

   c. V. D. Miller and S. F. Pellicori, "Ultraviolet Fluorescence Photography of the Shroud of Turin," *Journal of Biological Photography* 49, no. 3 (July 1981): 71–85.

   d. S. F. Pellicori and R. A. Chandos, "Portable Unit Permits UV/Vis Study of Shroud," *Industrial Research and Development* (February 1981): 186–189.

e. R. A. Morris, L. A. Schwalbe, and J. R. London, "X-ray Fluorescence Investigation of the Shroud of Turin," *X-Ray Spectrometry* 9, no. 2 (April 1980): 40–47.

f. J. H. Heller and A. D. Adler, "Blood on the Shroud of Turin," *Applied Optics* 19, no. 16 (August 15, 1980): 2742–2744.

g. E. J. Jumper and R. W. Mottern, "Scientific Investigation of the Shroud of Turin," *Applied Optics* 19, no. 12 (June 15, 1980): 1909–1912.

h. S. F. Pellicori, "Spectral Properties of the Shroud of Turin," *Applied Optics* 19, no. 12 (June 15, 1980): 1913–1920.

i. J. S. Accetta and J. S. Baumgart, "Infrared Reflectance Spectroscopy and Thermographic Investigations of the Shroud of Turin," *Applied Optics* 19, no. 12 (June 15, 1980): 1921–1929.

j. Roger Gilbert and Marion Gilbert, "Ultraviolet-Visible Reflectance and Fluorescence Spectra of the Shroud of Turin," *Applied Optics* 19, no. 12 (June 15, 1980): 1930–1936.

k. R. W. Mottern, R. J. London, and R. A. Morris, "Radiographic Examination of the Shroud of Turin — A Preliminary Report," *Materials Evaluation* 38, no. 12 (1979): 39–44.

l. V. Miller and D. Lynn, "De Lijkwade Van Turijn," *Natuur en Techniek* (February 1981): 102–125.

m. Robert Bucklin, "The Shroud of Turin: A Pathologist's Viewpoint," *Legal Medicine Annual* (1981).

n. S. Pellicori and M. Evans, "The Shroud of Turin through the Microscope," *Archaeology* 34, no. 1 (January–February 1981): 32–42.

4. Schwalbe and Rogers, "Physics and Chemistry of the Shroud of Turin," op. cit., 31:

There has been no evidence found to suggest that the visible image results from a colored foreign material on the cloth. In this regard, the data are quite internally consistent. Microscopic studies have revealed the image to be highly superficial; the image resides in the topmost fibers of the woven material as a translucent yellow discoloration. No pigment particles can be resolved by direct Shroud observation at 50x magnification, nor can unambiguously identified pigment particles be found on the tape samples at 1,000x. Microchemical studies of yellow fibrils taken from tape samples of the pure-image area have shown no indication for the presence of dyes, stains, inorganic pigments, or protein-, starch-, or wax-based painting media. X-ray fluorescence shows no detectable difference in elemental composition between image and non-image areas. Spectrophotometric reflectance reveals none of the characteristic spectral features of pigments or dyes. Ultraviolet fluorescence shows no indication of aromatic dyes or aromatic amino acids that might be expected from animal-collagen pigment binders. Direct visual observations of image areas that intersect scorch and water stains reveal nothing that might suggest the presence of organic dyes or water- protein-, or starch-based painting media.

5. McCrone's four articles:

   a. Walter C. McCrone and C. Skirius, "Light Microscopical Study of the Turin 'Shroud' I," *The Microscope* 28, no. 3 (1980): 105–113.

   b. Walter C. McCrone, "Light Microscopical Study of the Turin 'Shroud' II," *The Microscope* 28, no. 4 (1980): 115–128.

   c. Walter C. McCrone, "Microscopical Study of the Turin 'Shroud' III," *The Microscope* 29, no. 1 (1981): 19–39.

   d. Walter C. McCrone, "The Shroud of Turin: Blood or Artist's Pigment?" *Accounts of Chemical Research* 23, no. 3 (1990): 77–87.

6. Scientific reviews of McCrone's articles:

   a. Pellicori and Evans, "The Shroud of Turin through the Microscope," op. cit., 42.

b. Schwalbe and Rogers, "Physics and Chemistry of the Shroud of Turin," op. cit., 11–16.

c. Jackson, Jumper, and Ercoline, "Correlation of Image Intensity on the Turin Shroud with the 3-D Structure of a Human Body Shape," op. cit., 2251–2253.

d. Eric Jumper et al., "A Comprehensive Examination of the Various Stains and Images on the Shroud of Turin," in *Archaeological Chemistry III*, ed. by J. Lambert, *Advances in Chemistry*, vol. 205 (Washington, D.C.: American Chemical Society, 1984), 447–476.

e. Heller and Adler, "A Chemical Investigation of the Shroud of Turin," op. cit., 81–103.

f. Personal communication from Jumper and Adler concerning article "17-d," p. 468: "Under the experimental conditions employed in the X-ray investigation on the shroud, unfortunately iron would not be expected to show images as was implied in the review article. However, vermilion (mercuric sulfide, HgS) would be seen."

g. For the reader who is scientifically inclined, I would suggest carefully reading McCrone's article "16-d," Adler's article "17-e," and Jumper's article "17-d" so that you may decide for yourself, at the microscopic and chemical level, whether or not the shroud is a painting. To fully comprehend McCrone's article, you need to review the colored pictures in his article.

7. Heller and Adler, "Blood on the Shroud of Turin," op. cit., 2742. For those interested in reading more about the blood on the shroud, I suggest reading the work of Pierluigi Baima Bollone. His own bibliography is in his *Shroud Spectrum International* articles.

8. Heller and Adler, "A Chemical Investigation of the Shroud of Turin," op. cit., 81.

9. Among Adler's best articles are the following:

a. Heller and Adler, "A Chemical Investigation of the Shroud of Turin," op. cit.

b. Heller and Adler, "Blood on the Shroud of Turin," op. cit.

c. Jumper, Adler, et al., "A Comprehensive Examination of the Various Stains and Images on the Shroud of Turin," op. cit.

10. Schwalbe and Rogers, "Physics and Chemistry of the Shroud of Turin," op. cit., 36.

11. Pellicori and Evans, "The Shroud of Turin through the Microscope," op. cit., 41.

12. Schwalbe and Rogers, "Physics and Chemistry of the Shroud of Turin," op. cit., 11.

13. Heller and Adler, "A Chemical Investigation of the Shroud of Turin," op. cit., 81. "There is no chemical evidence for the application of any pigments, stains, or dyes on the cloth to produce the image found thereon. The chemical differences between image and non-image areas of the cloth indicate that the image was produced by some dehydrative oxidative process of the cellulose structure of the linen to yield a conjugated carbonyl group as the chromophore. However, a detailed mechanism for the production of this image, accounting for all of its properties, remains undetermined."

14. Articles describing the use of substances to produce yellowing of fibers are the following:

a. Heller and Adler, "A Chemical Investigation of the Shroud of Turin," op. cit., 98–99.

b. Pellicori, "Spectral Properties of the Shroud of Turin," op. cit., 1913–1920.

15. Four of the best articles describing the problems of the contact theory are the following:

a. Schwalbe and Rogers, "Physics and Chemistry of the Shroud of Turin," op. cit., 35. "If the image had been caused by the catalytic action of materials present on the corpse, direct contact of the body with the cloth seems to be the only likely material transfer mechanism. A general problem now becomes apparent. It would seem to follow that the dorsal image area was influenced by the weight of the body whereas the frontal image was imprinted only by the lesser weight of the covering cloth. Recall, however, that the densities at presumed contact points on both frontal and dorsal images do not differ significantly. These characteristics along with the superficial nature of the image would suggest that the contact transfer mechanism is pressure-independent. This apparent contradiction challenges not only the Pellicori-German model but most other hypotheses in this category."

b. Pellicori and Evans, "The Shroud of Turin through the Microscope," op. cit., 43.

c. Heller and Adler, "A Chemical Investigation of the Shroud of Turin," op. cit., 98–99.

d. Jumper, Adler, et. al., "A Comprehensive Examination of the Various Stains and Images on the Shroud of Turin," op. cit., 470. "The Shroud's mapping relationship, however, poses the strongest objection to a contact mechanism. Contact mechanisms have not been able to produce a convincing cloth-body distance relationship. In fact, taken alone, this mapping function seems to suggest some kind of a 'projection' mechanism, because there seems to be image present even where it does not appear to have been possible that the cloth was in contact with the body. We are left to identify what kind of 'projection' mechanism, and this we have been unable to do.

Simple molecular diffusion and 'radiation' models, for example, fail to account for the apparent resolution of the image as we understand it."

16. Jumper, Adler, et. al., "A Comprehensive Examination of the Various Stains and Images on the Shroud of Turin," op. cit., 451.

17. Jackson, Jumper, and Ercoline, "Correlation of Image Intensity on the Turin Shroud with the 3-D Structure of a Human Body Shape" op. cit., 2244–2270.

18. No mechanism is known that will reproduce the body-to-cloth transfer. The following articles discuss this:

a. John Jackson, Eric Jumper, and William Ercoline, "Correlation of Image Intensity on the Turin Shroud with the 3-D Structure of a Human Body Shape," *Applied Optics* 23, no. 14 (July 15, 1984): 2244–2270.

b. Schwalbe and Rogers, "Physics and Chemistry of the Shroud of Turin," op. cit., 35.

c. Heller and Adler, "A Chemical Investigation of the Shroud of Turin," op. cit., 99.

19. Jumper, Adler, et. al., "A Comprehensive Examination of the Various Stains and Images on the Shroud of Turin," op. cit., 460.

20. Ibid., 447–476.

21. Ibid., 450–451, and verbal communication with Jumper regarding wicking.

22. Ibid., 450 and 459.

23. Pellicori and Evans, "The Shroud of Turin through the Microscope," op. cit., 41. *(Personal communication with Jumper:* The image fibers penetrated the thread one fiber deep and possibly in some places, two fibers deep, even though it says three to four fibers deep on page 41 of Pellicori's article.)

24. Jumper, Adler, et. al., "A Comprehensive Examination of the Various Stains and Images on the Shroud of Turin," op. cit., 451.

25. G. Fanti et al., "Microscopic and Macroscopic Characteristics of the Shroud of Turin Image Superficiality," *Journal of Imaging Science and Technology* 54, no. 4 (July 2010): 40201-1–40201-8.

26. P. Di Lazzaro and D. Murra, "Shroud Like Coloration of Linen, Conservation Measures and Perception of Patterns onto the Shroud of Turin" *SHS Web of Conferences* 15 (2015), https://doi.org/10.1051/shsconf/20151500005.

27. Paolo Di Lazzaro, "Linen Coloration by Pulsed Radiation: A Review" (lecture presented at the International Conference on the Shroud of Turin, Pasco, Washington, July 22, 2017,).

Note 5.1: More on Vernon Miller and His Photographs of the Shroud of Turin

Vernon Miller, a professional scientific photographer, was a professor and the head of the Industrial and Scientific Department of the Brooks Institute of Photography in Santa Barbara, California, for approximately twenty-five years. Vernon participated as the official scientific photographer of the Shroud of Turin Research Project of 1978.

Because of Vernon's work in Turin and the gift of his collection, we now have access to his beautiful 4 x 5 and 8 x 10 black-and-white positives and negatives, and color transparencies of the shroud. A few examples from his collection can be seen in this book. He captured many 4 x 5 color transparencies under ultraviolet light for the scientific purpose of studying the shroud's cloth, blood, image, and more. He also took many 35-millimeter color micrographs ranging from 6x to 64x magnification of blood marks, body image, scorch marks, burn marks, water marks, wax, and the clear cloth of the shroud. It was because of Vernon's photographic expertise that we now have microscopic views of the shroud that allow us to see and better understand the shroud image at its fiber depth.

Comparing the shroud as it appears to the naked eye with the black-and-white negative film, we can see that it is only from the negative photo of the black-and-white film that we are able to appreciate the definite positive view of the man of the shroud. In his collection, there are many 4 x 5 and 8 x 10 black-and-white films, which illustrate Vernon's photographic and darkroom expertise. He used different exposure times and so forth to produce very fine black-and-white negative photos of high contrast that resulted in the clearest features of the hidden man of the shroud.

In summary, through his 35-millimeter micrographs of the shroud image fibers, the unique building blocks of the image are revealed. Through his ultraviolet light color transparencies, he has revealed a more precise imagery of the wounds and blood marks of the man of the shroud. There is much to be learned from these UV films. Moreover, through his high-contrast negatives, he has brought to light some of the clearest and most magnificent positive images of the man of the shroud. It is no wonder that Vernon exclaimed in a moment of awe, "What do you do with images like these?"[1] His generous response was to wish to have his collection digitized so that these exquisite images would be available to future generations. Since 2019, Vernon's extensive shroud collection has been available worldwide at shroudphotos.com, fulfilling Miller's wish.

At the website, most of the photos in Vernon Miller's collection can be enlarged (magnified) online. Many photos can be enlarged enough to easily examine the weave of the cloth. This is especially true for the larger black-and-white 8 x 10 films and color transparencies. Moreover, each photo can be downloaded and printed, resulting in a quality picture. These downloads are available for free, provided that the user follows the rules of the website's license. The intention of the website is to have Vernon Miller's photographs of the Shroud of Turin accessible to the public worldwide.

REFERENCES FOR NOTE 5.1

1. "Home Page," https://shroudphotos.com/.

Note 5.2: For Hypotheses on Image Formation

For years, major efforts have been made to understand the process of image formation: the mechanism that can reproduce this body-to-cloth image transfer. What image-formation mechanism brought about this chemical change of the topmost flax fibers that produced the negative image of the crucified man of the shroud? This chemical change — yellowing of the fibers — has indeed been caused by some physical event that is presently undetermined. I turned to Robert Rucker, a physicist who has been working diligently on shroud image formation and is exceedingly better qualified than I, to summarize the current hypotheses of image formation. He graciously sent me the following summary:

> In 1978, the Shroud of Turin Research Project (STURP) performed experiments on the Shroud to determine how the images were formed. These experiments led them to conclude that the full-size front and dorsal (back) images of a crucified man were not formed on the Shroud by pigment, a scorch, any liquid, or photography. How then were the images formed? Many if not most Shroud researchers now believe the images were formed by radiation. Some researchers (John Jackson, Mark Antonacci) argue that gravity and an air pressure difference resulting from the disappearance of the body would have caused the Shroud to collapse into the volume previously occupied by the body, where the cloth encountered radiation that discolored the fibers.

Other researchers believe a collapse of the cloth was not involved in image formation, but that the images were formed by radiation that exited the body and discolored the fibers when it hit the cloth. Paolo Di Lazzaro, based on his laser experiments, believes this radiation was probably ultraviolet light emitted from the body in an extremely brief energetic pulse, with the fibers being discolored by the ultraviolet light in a photo-chemical reaction. Giulio Fanti hypothesizes this radiation was charged particles emitted perpendicular from each point on the body, with their path to the cloth controlled by a vertically oriented electrostatic field. Bob Rucker hypothesizes the images were formed by vertically collimated radiation, predominately charged particles, that were emitted homogeneously in the body. These charged particles caused an electrical discharge from the top fibers facing the body that discolored the fibers by heat deposited in the thin outer layer of the fibers and/or chemical attack by ozone produced by the electrical discharge."[1] [John Jackson,[2] Mark Antonacci,[3] Paolo Di Lazzaro,[4] Giulio Fanti,[5,6] Bob Rucker[7]]

In summary, the two main features of the present hypotheses are (1) the body image was formed by some kind of "radiation" and (2) the source of the radiation involved the body. These hypothesized events have never been known to occur to any dead body. In conclusion, microscopic chemical data and ongoing research continue to point to a unique event of image formation.

REFERENCES FOR NOTE 5.2

1. Personal communication from Robert Rucker.

2. John Jackson's hypothesis is found at his website: www.ShroudofTurin.com.

3. Mark Antonacci, "Particle Radiation from the Body Could Explain the Shroud's Images and Its Carbon Dating," *Scientific Research and Essays* 7, no. 29 (July 2012): 2613–2623.

4. Paolo Di Lazzaro, "Linen Coloration by Pulsed Radiation: A Review" (lecture presented at the International Conference on

the Shroud of Turin, Pasco, Washington, July 22, 2017, https://www.academia.edu/38029774).

5.   G. Fanti, "Hypotheses regarding the Formation of the Body Image on the Turin Shroud: A Critical Compendium," *Journal of Imaging Science and Technology* 55, no. 6, November–December 2011): 1–14.

6.   G. Fanti et al, "Experimental Results Using Corona Discharge to Attempt to Reproduce the Turin Shroud Image," *SHS Web of Conferences* 15 (2015), https://doi.org/10.1051/shsconf/20151500003. Note: Giulio Fanti has also been exploring the "Holy Fire" to see if its effects may have any relationship to the Turin Shroud. The Holy Fire has been recorded annually at least for the past twelve hundred years at Holy Sepulchre (Church of the Resurrection) of Jerusalem. For more information, see Fanti's article: Giulio Fanti, "Is the Holy Fire Related to the Turin Shroud?" *Global Journal of Archaeology and Anthropology* 10, no. 2 (2019): 21–30, https://juniperpublishers.com/gjaa/pdf/GJAA.MS.ID.555782.pdf.

7.   Bob Rucker's hypothesis is found at his website: www.shroudresearch.net.

Chapter 6: Buried according to the Jewish Burial Custom

1.   *The Mishnah,* trans. by Herbert Danby (Oxford: Oxford University Press, 1933), Second Division, Moed. Tractate: Shabbath, 23[5], 120.

2.   Maurice Lamm, *The Jewish Way in Death and Mourning* (New York: Jonathan David Publishers, 1969), 6–7.

3.   Ibid., 244.

4.   Solomon Ganzfried, *Code of Jewish Law: Kitzur Shulchan Aruch,* trans. by Hyman E. Goldin (New York: Hebrew Publishing Company, 1963) vol. 4, ch. 197, *The Purification, Shrouds, and Utilization of Anything Belonging to the Dead* (Tahara), nos. 9 and 10, 99–100.

5. *The Mishnah,* op. cit., introduction, XIII.

6. *The Mishnah,* op. cit., Third Division, Nashim. Tractate: Nazir, 7^2, 289–290.

7. Ibid., Sixth Division, Tohoroth. Tractate: Oholoth, 3^5, 653–654.

8. Ibid., appendix II: Money, Weights, and Measures, 798.

9. Ibid., Third Division, Nashim. Tractate: Nazir, 7^2, 290.

10. Ganzfried, *Code of Jewish Law,* op. cit., 99.

11. Ibid., 100.

12. *The Mishnah,* op. cit., Fifth Division, Kodashim. Tractate: Zebahim, 3^1, note 4, 471.

13. Bonnie Lavoie, Gilbert Lavoie, et al., "In Accordance with Jewish Burial Custom, the Body of Jesus Was Not Washed," *Sindon* (December 1981): 19–29. Also published in *Shroud Spectrum International 1*, no. 3 (June 1982): 8–17, https://www.shroud.com/spectrum.htm, and *The Biblical Archeologist 45, no. 1* (Winter 1982): 5–6, https://www.jstor.org/stable/i361060.

14. The contents of this chapter 6 on Jewish burial customs previously had been published in my first book, Gilbert R. Lavoie, *Unlocking the Secrets of the Shroud* (Allen, Texas: Thomas More, 1998). One of the comments on the cover of my first book was from Jacob Neusner, Distinguished Research Professor of Religious Studies, University of South Florida, and Bard College. Concerning the chapter on Jewish burial customs he said, "The discussion of the burial rites of Judaism is informed and illuminating."

Note: 6.1: Quotes from the Abridged Version of the Sixteenth-Century Code of Jewish Law

1. *If a person falls and dies instantly, if his body was bruised and blood flowed from the wound, and there is apprehension that his life-blood was absorbed in his clothes, he should not be ritually cleansed, but interred in his garments and shoes. He should be wrapped in a sheet, above his garments. That sheet is called sobeb. It is customary to scoop up the earth at the spot where he fell, and*

if blood happens to be there or near by, all that earth is buried with him. Only the garments which he wore when he fell are buried with him, but if the blood splashed on other garments, or if he was placed upon pillows and sheets while the blood was flowing, all these need not be buried with him, but they must be thoroughly washed until no trace of blood remains, and the water is poured into the grave. If, however, the deceased did not bleed at all, his clothes should be removed, his body cleansed and wrapped in shrouds, as is done in the case of a natural death. . . .

2. *If blood has flown from the injured body, but it stopped and his clothes were removed, after which he recovered and lived for a few days and then died, he must be cleansed and dressed in shrouds. Even if his body is stained with the blood which issued forth from him, he must be cleansed, for the blood lost while being alive is not to be regarded as life-blood; we are only concerned with the blood which one loses while dying, for it is likely that this was his life-blood, or it is possible that life-blood was mixed with it.*[1]

References for Note 6.1

1. Solomon Ganzfried, *Code of Jewish Law: Kitzur Shulchan Aruch,* trans. by Hyman E. Goldin (New York: Hebrew Publishing Company, 1963) vol. 4, ch. 197, *The Purification, Shrouds, and Utilization of Anything Belonging to the Dead* (Tahara), nos. 9 and 10, 99–100.

Chapter 7: The Transfer of Blood to Linen Cloth

1. Vernon Miller and S. F. Pellicori, "Ultraviolet Fluorescence Photography of the Shroud of Turin," *Journal of Biological Photography* 49, no. 3 (July 1981): 84.

2. There is medical consensus that the source of the blood/fluid that resulted in the small of the back blood mark was from the open chest wound. However, there have been ongoing hypotheses as to how the blood arrived at the small of the back. No qualitative and quantitative experiments have yet

established exactly how this occurred, partly due to the many unknown factors surrounding the event. For example, if the blood had been in the pleural cavity of the chest, was it still able to clot on skin? How liquid or viscous was the blood/fluid as it flowed from the wound? What was the position of the body when the event occurred? Was it when he was placed on the cloth or when he was being carried to the tomb? Did the fire destroy the data?

3. Pierre Barbet, *A Doctor at Calvary* (New York: Doubleday, 1953), 24.

4. The position of the blood clot of the chest wound is another confirmation that the man of the shroud died in the vertical position.

5. Clara Davidsohn and Minnie Wells, *Todd-Sanford Clinical Diagnosis by Laboratory Methods* (Philadelphia: W. B. Saunders,1962), 330.

6. Gilbert Lavoie et al., "Blood on the Shroud of Turin: Part II," *Shroud Spectrum International,* no. 8 (September 1983): 2–10, https://www.shroud.com/spectrum.htm.

7. Davidsohn and Wells, op. cit., 346.

8. Ibid., 332.

9. Shock from severe blood loss and decrease in vascular volume result in some of the following signs and symptoms: pale, cold, clammy (sweaty) skin, low blood pressure, rapid heartbeat, shallow rapid breathing. If untreated, poorly perfused tissues become hypoxic, and multiple organ failure occurs, followed by death.

10. *The Mishnah,* trans. by Herbert Danby (Oxford: Oxford University Press, 1933), Second Division, Moed. Tractate: Shabbath, 23^5, 120.

11. The 1995 Israeli Calendar, published by the Government Press Office, Jerusalem, Israel, obtained from the Israeli Consulate, Boston, Massachusetts.

12. *The Mishnah,* op. cit., Sixth Division, Tohoroth. Tractate: Oholoth, 3^5, 653–654.

13. Barbet, op. cit., 24–25.

Note 7.1: More on the Importance of Moisture on Clot-to-Cloth Transfer

There are very few blood marks that are smudged on the shroud.[1] Moreover, when comparing scourge marks of the front of the body to the back, the details and contrast are "only slightly less prominent on the front than on the dorsal image, indicating that the large difference in weight for each side had only minor influence on the imprinting of the scourges."[2] A very adequate answer as to why there were few smudges and that the weight of the body had very little influence on imprinting of the scourges lies in the fact that the transfers of blood and serum from body to cloth are dependent on the available moisture. Once that moisture is soaked up into the cloth, there is almost no ability to further transfer blood to cloth.

In the study of blood clots to cloth in chapter 7, it was noted that the transfers occurred quickly. This *quick transfer of blood* can be more easily understood by doing a simple experiment. First, create a pool of water by placing nine drops of water on an impermeable countertop. Second, place a linen cloth over the drop and count the seconds for the complete absorption of the moisture. One sees that the time is very short. *Instantly, the moisture begins to soak through the cloth.* Within the first five seconds, most of the moisture is soaked up and by ten seconds, there is very little moisture left on the counter for further transfer. By twenty seconds, the counter is dry. Therefore, not weight but the amount of moisture is what is most important in making the transfer. And this also explains why smudges did not occur once the cloth was placed over the body. Furthermore, it is evident that those who buried the body took great care in not only taking the body down from the cross but also in placing the cloth over the body so as to not disturb the moist, fragile blood clots. Again, all of this suggests that this was a Jewish burial (see chapter 6).

References on Note 7.1

1.   Vernon Miller and S. F. Pellicori, "Ultraviolet Fluorescence Photography of the Shroud of Turin," *Journal of Biological Photography* 49, no. 3 (July 1981): 80. Possible smudge on the back of the head.

2.   Ibid., 84–85.

Note 7.2: More on Blood Clots and Serum

As I continued to study the subtleties of the shroud's blood marks, I began to realize that the serum from the clots on the man of the shroud did not all drip away as it did on the vertical plastic surface experiment, but rather some of it clung to the skin. Examples are the serum lines seen as halos around the blood marks of the wrist and chest wounds using ultraviolet fluorescence photography (figure note 7.2).

These serum lines, like the serum lines of the first plastic surface experiment (figure 7.9), tell another part of the story. Crucifixion, as noted in the Mishnah, was a dynamic, ongoing process of blood dripping or gushing from the crucified. The blood flowed from an open wound onto the surface of the skin, where it would clot, exude serum, and eventually dry up. But if life was maintained, bleeding from the open wounds would continue to flow onto the skin of the body. All of the serum did not drain away as it did in my simple plastic surface experiment, but some did accumulate on the skin adjacent to the clots. When death finally came, the last blood flows of the wrist clotted and then retracted, the exuded serum clung to the adjacent skin, and the residual serum kept the clot moist, allowing its image to be

Figure Note 7.2: UV fluorescence photography of wrist and chest wounds showing serum exudates as halos

Wrist wound with halos   *Chest wound with halos*

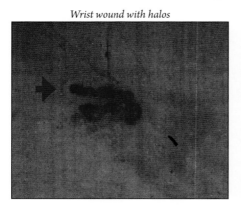
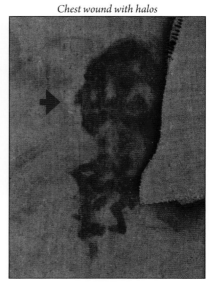

transferred to cloth. Details like this help us to appreciate that the blood marks of the shroud represent mirror images of clotted blood. Paint cannot separate and create the serum lines that are seen here (figure note 7.2). Only blood does this.

When I called Vern Miller in 1991 to ask him for some shroud photos, he reminded me of the work he had done in 1978 regarding the blood marks. Using ultraviolet fluorescence photography, he took pictures of the shroud and found that there were halos of fluorescence around some of the blood marks.[1] For example, there were "clear fluorescing borders around the hand [wrist] wound blood stains."[2] He went on to say that he was never able to reproduce his findings using blood. In our discussion, I realized that he had not photographed any new experimental blood samples with serum lines. In response, I sent Miller the blood marks with serum lines (example, figure 7.9), which were the result of my earlier transfer experiments. He took pictures of these using an ultraviolet fluorescent light source and found that the blood marks with the serum lines did indeed fluoresce, reproducing the fluorescent halos that he had found around some of the blood marks of the shroud. Vernon Miller photographically confirmed what Dr. Barbet had visualized forty-five years before: the presence of clot exudates (serum) on the shroud.

In summary, what does the study of these blood clots and serum tell us about the man of the shroud? In Dr. Barbet's words, "there is no flow of blood on the Shroud; there are only the counter drawings of clots; these clots represent that part of the blood which has congealed on the skin, while flowing over it. If I sometimes refer to flows of blood, when describing the shroud, it is because these clots tell us of the past when that blood flowed on the skin."[3] From the study of these mirror images of blood clots, we know that in the past the man of the shroud died in the position of crucifixion (chapters 8). And they tell us much more.

REFERENCES ON NOTE 7.2

1. Vernon Miller and S. F. Pellicori, "Ultraviolet Fluorescence Photography of the Shroud of Turin," *Journal of Biological Photography* 49, no. 3 (July 1981): 75.

2. Ibid., 82.

3. Pierre Barbet, *A Doctor at Calvary* (New York: Doubleday, 1953), 28.

Chapter 8: Reconfirming That the Man of the Shroud Died in a Crucified Position

1. *The Mishnah,* trans. by Herbert Danby (Oxford: Oxford University Press, 1933), Sixth Division, Tohoroth, Tractate: Oholoth, 3^5, 654.

2. The small blood mark seen just distal to the off-image blood mark in figure 8.2 was likely formed during a very *quick transfer of blood* (see note 7.1) during the cloth's very short contact with the moist blood clot as the cloth touched that clot for an instant and continued to pass on as the cloth was draped over the side of the body (figure 8.5).

3. Gilbert Lavoie et al., "Blood on the Shroud of Turin: Part I," *Shroud Spectrum International,* no. 7 (June 1983): 15–19, https://www.shroud.com/spectrum.htm.

Note 8.1: More on Mock Blood Flows

A mock blood flow of the chest wound was done on the volunteer while in position 2. As a result of the volunteer's position, the mock blood flow dripped off the body at a point that was nearly identical in length with the blood mark of the chest wound seen on the shroud. It was consistent with the final position 2 of death.

Finally, a mock blood flow of the blood flowing from the left wrist was done while the volunteer was moving back and forth between position 1 and position 2. The blood flow coming down his forearm developed into a series of zigzag patterns because of the back-and-forth movement of his body between the two positions. Similar blood mark patterns are seen on the forearms of the man of the shroud. (Note: During the day, after a volunteer accumulated well over two hours of being on the cross, it was observed that he could bend his head forward only slightly due to the muscle tightness of his upper back and neck.)

Chapter 9: Blood Marks on the Face

1. Gilbert Lavoie, Bonnie Lavoie, and Alan Adler, "Blood on the Shroud of Turin: Part III, the Blood on the Face," *Shroud Spectrum International,* no. 20 (September 1986): 3–6, https://www.shroud.com/spectrum.htm.

2. The blood marks of the shroud are collectively consistent with a cloth that was draped/wrapped and sufficiently tucked to make contact with moist blood/blood clots that flowed from or were on the body of a man who had been scourged and crucified. The off-image blood mark (chapter 8) and the blood marks of the face (chapter 9) are two examples of this consistency. Another example is observed on the back image of the shroud; the right and left footprints in blood likely occurred during wrapping when that end of the cloth was moved upward onto the moist blood/blood clots of the flexed crossed feet. Most important, the explanation of this posterior wrapping of the feet is consistent with the observed anatomical positions of the legs and feet of the image. These and other blood marks helped to determine and confirm the three-dimensional anatomy of the image.

Chapter 10: The Image of an Upright Man

1. This study was presented at the 1989 Paris International Shroud Symposium (unpublished paper). It was later published in my first book, *Unlocking the Secrets of the Shroud* (Allen, Texas: Thomas More, 1998). Other chapters from my first book, with revisions and additions as needed, are also included in whole or in part in chapters 4 through 10 of this book.

2. G. Lavoie, "Turin Shroud: A Medical Forensic Study of Its Blood Marks and Image" (published at the Proceedings of the International Workshop on the Scientific Approach to the Acheiropoietos Images, ENEA, Frascati, Italy, May 4–6, 2010, http://www.acheiropoietos.info/proceedings/LavoieWeb.pdf).

3. Raymond Brown, *The Gospel according to John,* vol. 29 (I–XII) and vol. 29A (XIII–XXI) (New York: Doubleday, 1986), CXV in introduction.

4. Ibid., 146.

5. *Ignatius Catholic Study Bible* (San Francisco: Ignatius Press, 2001), 186n12:32, 166n3:14.

Note 10.1: More on Observations

The comparison of the light areas of the original negative shroud image to the negative image of a volunteer with light coming from above is not related to any hypothesis of image formation. The comparison is simply an observation (see chapter 5, note 5.2 for information on hypotheses of image formation).

Light in our world is generally from above. This light is the cause of the shadows that we see on faces and so forth. These daily experiences develop our general perception of how we see people in our world. In other words, light from above casts shadows that we are familiar with in daily life. When we stand in the light of day, shadows are cast upon us in a different way than when we are lying down (supine). In contrast, if light comes from below, people appear strange and even frightening because it is not our normal perception of what we look like (think of a flashlight shining up under a face in a dark room).

The comparison of the negative photograph of the volunteer to the negative shroud image on the cloth was the first step in discovering that the man of the shroud is in the upright position. The upright position of the image of the man was then established by anatomical observations related to gravity. They, too, are also part of our daily experiences. What happens to long hair if one is upright as opposed to being supine? What happens to body form if one is upright as opposed to being supine? There are no hypotheses presented here. These observations are simply what is evident.

The shroud image, a product of an event that continues to remain scientifically unexplained, was created with certain inherent characteristics that we can now observe. Photography remains one of the best visual tools that we have for observing these characteristics.

Note: 10.2: More on Flattening of the Anatomical Form

Rigor mortis has often been discussed in relation to the shroud image. The following gives some perspective on any discussion regarding rigor mortis. Rigor mortis is the temporary rigidity of muscles occurring after death. It has no effect on the overlying fat and skin, which are easily flattened, even during rigor mortis. Rigor mortis usually peaks in four to six hours after death, tapers off thereafter, and is mostly gone within twenty-four hours. It is absent after thirty-six hours. In rigor mortis, the rigidity of the muscles runs on a scale over time from the condition of no rigidity and increases to full rigidity; then from its peak it scales down through less rigidity, which is easy to break, to soft and weak rigidity, to complete resolution. As rigidity decreases, the force of gravity always dominates. Because of body weight, bodies in autopsy rooms all have flattening of skin, fat, and muscle, resulting in loss of dorsal body form.

In summary, rigor mortis is the biological event of muscle rigidity that occurs after death for a short period of time as described above.

Why do we see what appears to be a three-dimensional figure on a two-dimensional (flat) surface? From an artistic or photographic perspective, an image's form is dependent on variation of value. Variation of value is the variation of shading that causes the eye to decipher form.

Figure note 10.2 shows the figures of a cylinder and a rectangle. On the left we have a cylinder that has form because it has many shades of gray from white to black. The cylinder on the left looks like a three-dimensional cylinder because it has variation of shading. On the right we have a rectangle that has no form because it contains only one shade of gray. More specifically, the rectangle on the right is flat. It is two-dimensional with no depth. It has no form because the entire surface has the same shading.

By studying the effects of gravity at the surface contact points of a body lying in the supine position (back is down), we understand how body weight affects anatomical form. From the following study we can appreciate the complexity of dorsal image formation. Figure 10.9 is a drawing of a male volunteer who has the

Figure Note 10.2: The grayscale of form

Cylinder   Rectangle

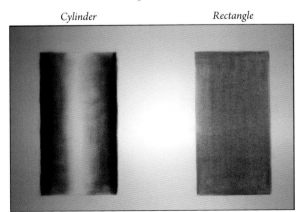

On the left we have what is perceived as a cylinder in that it has form. The many shades of gray from white to black (grayscale of form) give it its form. On the right we have a rectangle that has no form because it contains only one shade of gray. It is perceived as being flat.

anatomical form that we would expect to see of someone in the upright position. Figure 10.10 is the same man now lying on his back on a large plate of glass, and we are looking at him from below. The weight of his body has flattened his backside, and there are areas of the back and buttocks and calves that have lost their roundness (form) from when he was standing. The flat areas are similar to the flat rectangle of figure note 10.2 that has no form. You would see the same loss of body form if you were to examine bodies in an autopsy room. In figure 10.10, also note the change of the hair flow from the upright position to the supine position. In the supine position the weight of the hair and the weight of the body against the hair cause it to flatten.

Much of the above comes directly from my article "Turin Shroud: A Medical Forensic Study of Its Blood Marks and Image."[1] For further information on the flattening of the backside of a corpse and for references on the rigor mortis of the body, see this same article referenced below.

REFERENCES ON NOTE 10.2

1. G. Lavoie, "Turin Shroud: A Medical Forensic Study of Its Blood Marks and Image" (published at the Proceedings of the International Workshop on the Scientific Approach to the Acheiropoietos Images, ENEA, Frascati, Italy, May 4–10, 2010).

Chapter 11: John's Tomb Narrative: What Did He See, What Did He Believe?

1. Richard Bauckham, *God Crucified: Monotheism and Christology in the New Testament*, (Grand Rapids, MI: William Eerdmans Publishing, 1989), 50.

Chapter 12: God Is at Work

1. Raymond Brown, *The Gospel according to John*, vol. 29 (I–XII) and vol. 29A (XIII–XXI) (New York: Doubleday, 1986), 526. "Jesus himself consistently refers to them [miracles] as 'works.'"

Chapter 13: The Revelation of the Spirit

1. Raymond Brown, *The Gospel according to John,* vol. 29 (I–XII) and vol. 29A (XIII–XXI) (New York: Doubleday, 1986).

2. Ibid., 517–518.

3. Ibid., 711.

4. Ibid., 994. Jesus is in the process of ascending.

5. Ibid., 1011–1017. For more on the ascension of Jesus.

Chapter 14: Who God Is

Note 14.1: More on the Man Blind from Birth

The healed man's response to the Pharisees who questioned him tells the rest of the story. From the healed man's perspective, the source of the power that enabled him to see is summarized in his following answer to the Pharisees, "Never since the world began has it been heard that anyone open the eyes of a person born blind. If this man were not from God, he could do nothing" (John 9:32–33).

Similarly, from the perspective of searching for the source of the power that created the shroud image, the healed blind man's answer to the Pharisees gives us this parallel perspective; this sign/work, too, is beyond our concept of space and time: Never since the world began has it been heard that any dead person has left an image like we see on the shroud. If the dead man of the shroud were not from God, he could do nothing.

1. Raymond Brown, *The Gospel according to John,* vol. 29 (I–XII) and vol. 29A (XIII–XXI) (New York: Doubleday, 1986), 499. "The use of the term aletheia, [truth,] in this Gospel [John] rests upon common Hellenistic usage in which it hovers between the meanings of 'reality,' or 'the ultimately real,' and 'knowledge of the real.'"

Chapter 15: The Hour of Glory

1. Raymond Brown, *The Gospel according to John,* vol. 29 (I–XII) and vol. 29A (XIII–XXI) (New York: Doubleday, 1986), 1013. Jesus tells his disciples over and over again that he is going to his Father (John 14:12, 28) (John 16:5, 10, 28).

2. Ibid., 146 and 348. "I AM. This is one of the four relatively clear instances of the absolute use of *ego eimi* without a predicate implied (see App IV.). Some have suggested that 'Son of Man' is the implied predicate, but it does not fit John's thought that the ultimate insight into the exalted Jesus would be that he is Son of Man. The exalted Jesus as confessed as Lord and God in xx 28, and our reading of the divine use of *ego eimi* here fits in with that estimation."

3. Ibid., 146.

Chapter 16: The Bread of God

No references.

◇◇◇◇◇◇◇◇◇

Illustration Credits

PHOTOS USED WITHIN text are used with permission and copyright protection of the following:

Copyright 1978 Vernon Miller (permission granted by the D'Muhala and Lavoie Trust, 2019, and Tom D'Muhala), Copyright 2022 Gilbert R. Lavoie, Copyright 2021 Giulio Fanti, Copyright 2022 Camile Vicenti

Copyright 1978 Vernon Miller: Photo for the book cover, figures 1.1, 1.2, 1.3, 1.5, 1.6, 2.1, 2.2, 2.3, 2.4, 3.1, 3.2, 3.3, 3.4, 3.5, 3.6, 3.7, 3.8, 3.9, 3.10, 3.11, 3.12, 3.13, 3.14, 5.1, 5.2, 5.3, 5.4, 6.1, 6.2, 6.3, 6.4, 6.5, 6.6, 7.1, 7.2, 7.3, 7.4, 7.5, 7.6, 7.7, 7.8, 8.1, 8.2, 9.1, 10.1, 10.2, 10.3, 10.4, 10.5, 10.6, 10.7, 10.11, 10.12, 11.1, 12.1, 12.2, 12.4, 12.5, 14.1, 14.2, 16.1: front black-and-white image, 16.2: back black-and-white image, Figure Note 7.2 (permission granted by the D'Muhala and Lavoie Trust, 2019, and Tom D'Muhala)

Copyright 2022 Gilbert R. Lavoie: Figures 7.9, 7.10, 7.11, 7.12, 7.13, 8.3, 8.4, 8.5, 8.6, 8.7, 8.8 (8.7 and 8.8: manikin represents position of the volunteer documented by Bonnie Lavoie, and manikin was prepared and photographed with the assistance of William Cail), 9.2, 9.3, 9.4, 9.5, 9.6, 10.2,

10.3, 10.4, 10.6, 10.7, 10.8, 10.9, 10.10, 10.11, 12.3, Figure Note 10.2

About the Author

DR. GILBERT R. LAVOIE is a medical doctor, a specialist in internal medicine, occupational medicine, and public health. He has pursued a forensic and scriptural study of the Shroud of Turin for more than 40 years. He has published books, a video, and articles all related to scriptural and medical forensic studies of the blood marks and image of the man of the shroud. Dr. Lavoie, along with his colleague, Tom D'Muhala, digitized and organized some of the finest photographs of the Shroud of Turin done by Vernon Miller, who was the official scientific photographer of the 1978 Shroud of Turin Research Project. The Vernon Miller photo collection is now available worldwide on the internet at www.shroudphotos.com.

In the last several years Dr. Lavoie worked with the internationally known sculptor, Pablo Eduardo. Eduardo recently completed a bronze sculpture that is a three-dimensional replica of the image of the man of the Shroud of Turin. This was done in exquisite detail, paying much attention to the anatomy of the figure. This sculpture reveals a whole new way of understanding the shroud image.

Sophia Institute

Sophia Institute is a nonprofit institution that seeks to nurture the spiritual, moral, and cultural life of souls and to spread the gospel of Christ in conformity with the authentic teachings of the Roman Catholic Church.

Sophia Institute Press fulfills this mission by offering translations, reprints, and new publications that afford readers a rich source of the enduring wisdom of mankind.

Sophia Institute also operates the popular online Catholic resource CatholicExchange.com. *Catholic Exchange* provides world news from a Catholic perspective as well as daily devotionals and articles that will help readers to grow in holiness and live a life consistent with the teachings of the Church.

In 2013, Sophia Institute launched Sophia Institute for Teachers to renew and rebuild Catholic culture through service to Catholic education. With the goal of nurturing the spiritual, moral, and cultural life of souls, and an abiding respect for the role and work of teachers, we strive to provide materials and programs that are at once enlightening to the mind and ennobling to the heart; faithful and complete, as well as useful and practical.

Sophia Institute gratefully recognizes the Solidarity Association for preserving and encouraging the growth of our apostolate over the course of many years. Without their generous and timely support, this book would not be in your hands.

www.SophiaInstitute.com
www.CatholicExchange.com
www.SophiaInstituteforTeachers.org

Sophia Institute Press® is a registered trademark of Sophia Institute.
Sophia Institute is a tax-exempt institution as defined by the
Internal Revenue Code, Section 501(c)(3). Tax ID 22-2548708.